IT English
Listening and Speaking
中级IT英语听说教程

Intermediate
1

总 主 编 **司炳月**
分 册 主 编 **王晓华**
分册副主编 **张贵玫 黄 滔 张晓博**

清華大学出版社
北 京

内 容 简 介

为顺应经济全球化和信息技术的发展趋势，培养兼具 IT 专业技能和外语能力的人才，以适应 IT 行业发展需要，特编写了本教材。全书共有 16 个单元，每个单元分为 Section A、Section B 和 Section C 三大部分。其中，Section A 为听力训练，包含听前热身活动及与单元主题相关的精听练习，题目设置由易到难；Section B 为口语技巧讲解，并设有相关的思考问题及交流任务；Section C 为与国内外大型英语考试题型相近的听力测试，以便学生进一步练习和巩固听力技巧，题型多样，题量丰富。本书还配有相关的听力音频和课件资源，需要的读者请扫描正文第二页的二维码下载使用。

本书适合作为 IT 相关专业本科生和科技英语专业学生的英语听力教材，也可作为从事 IT 相关工作人士提升英语听说技能的参考资料。

版权所有，侵权必究。举报：010-62782989，beiqinquan@tup.tsinghua.edu.cn。

图书在版编目（CIP）数据

中级 IT 英语听说教程 . 1 / 司炳月总主编；王晓华分册主编 . —北京：清华大学出版社，2017（2021.8重印）

ISBN 978-7-302-47966-6

Ⅰ.①中…　Ⅱ.①司…　②王…　Ⅲ.① IT 产业 – 英语 – 听说教学 – 高等学校 – 教材　Ⅳ.① F49

中国版本图书馆 CIP 数据核字（2017）第 211296 号

责任编辑：刘　艳
封面设计：平　原
责任校对：王凤芝
责任印制：宋　林

出版发行：清华大学出版社
　　　　网　　址：http://www.tup.com.cn, http://www.wqbook.com
　　　　地　　址：北京清华大学学研大厦 A 座　　　邮　编：100084
　　　　社 总 机：010-62770175　　　　　　　　邮　购：010-62786544
　　　　投稿与读者服务：010-62776969, c-service@tup.tsinghua.edu.cn
　　　　质 量 反 馈：010-62772015, zhiliang@tup.tsinghua.edu.cn

印 装 者：三河市天利华印刷装订有限公司
经　　销：全国新华书店
开　　本：185mm×260mm　　印　张：14.25　　字　数：289 千字
版　　次：2017 年 8 月第 1 版　　　　　　　印　次：2021 年 8 月第 6 次印刷
定　　价：59.00元

产品编号：073634-03

中级 IT 英语听说教程 1

Intermediate IT English Listening and Speaking 1

编 写 组

总 主 编　**司炳月**

分 册 主 编　**王晓华**

分册副主编　**张贵玫　黄 滔　张晓博**

编　　　者　**王 健　吕飞莎　刘 欣　刘晓静　曹 放　曹 麟**
　　　　　　刘菁菁　邵 林　于 芳　张婉婷　张雅欣　宋 辉
　　　　　　王珞珈

　　本教材是 2016 年辽宁省社会科学规划基金项目"专门用途英语理论在大学英语教学中的实践与应用——基于辽宁省 IT 英语人才培养模式的研究"（项目编号：L16DYY005）的阶段性成果；是辽宁省教育科学"十三五"规划 2017 年度立项课题"IT 专门用途英语教材体系建设研究"（项目编号：JG17DB103）的阶段性成果；也是 2016 年国家社科基金项目"信息技术背景下中国外语学习环境'生态给养'转化有效性研究"（项目编号：16BYY093）的阶段性成果。

前言

一、编写背景

1. 《国家中长期教育改革和发展规划纲要（2010—2020 年）》

信息时代的悄然而至，使得我国教育在面临难得的改革与发展机遇的同时，也面临着全新的挑战。传统的教育教学理念、教育模式、教学内容、教学方式、教学手段、教育结构乃至整个教育体制都将随之发生变革。2010 年，教育部颁发了《国家中长期教育改革和发展规划纲要（2010—2020 年）》（以下简称《纲要》），《纲要》中提出要"优化学科专业、类型、层次结构，促进多学科交叉和融合。扩大应用型、复合型、技能型人才培养规模"。在对创新人才培养模式的论述中提出，要"加强教材建设，确定不同教育阶段学生必须掌握的核心内容，形成教学内容更新机制"。

2. 《全民科学素质行动计划纲要实施方案（2016—2020 年）》

2016 年 3 月，国务院办公厅印发了《全民科学素质行动计划纲要实施方案（2016—2020 年）》（以下简称《方案》）。《方案》中对高等教育中的教材要求有清楚的阐述："加强各类人群科技教育培训的教材建设。结合不同人群特点和需求，不断更新丰富科技教育培训的教材内容，注重培养具有创意、创新、创业能力的高层次创造性人才。将相关学科内容纳入各级各类科技教育培训教材和教学计划。"

3. 《大学英语教学指南》

《大学英语教学指南》（以下简称《指南》）是新时期普通高等学校制定大学英语教学大纲、进行大学英语课程建设、开展大学英语课程评价的依据。《指南》在对教材建设和教学资源的论述中明确阐述了："鼓励各高校建设符合本校定位与特点的大学英语校本数字化课程资源；鼓励本区域内同类高校跨校开发大学英语数字化课程资源。"

二、编写原则

本套教材是与 IT 及其相关专业密切相关的知识课程，符合新形势下国家对复合型人才培养提出的要求，符合语言学习规律和新时代大学生的认知水平，也满足大学生专业学习和未来职业发展的实际需要，有利于促进复合型人才培养目标的实现。本套教材在设计与编写过程中遵循以下原则：

1. 满足社会对于复合型人才培养的需求

当代大学生正面临多元化社会带来的冲突和挑战，复合型人才的培养成为国家、社会发展的需求。因此，为社会提供既具有专业知识又具备跨语言交际能力、能够直接参与国际交流与竞争的国际化通用型人才是高校人才培养的重点和难点，也是全球化对人才提出的更高、更新的要求。

2. 满足学生对于专业与外语知识相结合的需求

高校开设大学英语课程，一方面满足了国家、社会发展的需求，为国家改革开放和经济社会发展服务；另一方面，也满足了学生专业学习、国际交流、继续深造、工作就业等方面的需要。本套教材旨在满足 IT 及其相关专业学生的需求，帮助他们在掌握专业知识的同时提高英语水平。此外，教材亦体现了专门用途英语理论对大学英语教学课程设置的具体要求。

3. 满足大学英语教学大纲和教学目标的要求

大学英语的教学目标是培养学生的英语应用能力，增强学生的跨文化交际意识和交际能力；同时发展其自主学习能力，提高综合文化素养，使他们在学习、生活、社会交往和未来工作中能够有效地使用英语，满足国家、社会、学校和个人发展的需要。本套教材编写的目的就是使学生能够在 IT 专业领域中使用英语进行有效的交流；能够有效地运用有关篇章、语用等知识；能够较好地理解有一定语言难度、内容较为熟悉或与本人所学专业相关的口头或书面材料；能够对不同来源的信息进行综合、对比、分析，并得出自己的结论或形成自己的认识。

三、编写依据

1. "专业知识" + "外语能力" 的 "复合型" 人才培养目标

大学英语课程作为高等学校人文教育的一部分，兼具工具性和人文性。在进一步提高学生英语听、说、读、写、译基本能力的基础上，学生可以通过学习与专业或未来工作有关的学术英语或职业英语获得在学术或职业领域进行交流的相关能力。本套教材是根据大学英语教学大纲和教学目标的要求，采用系统、科学的教材编写原则和方法编写而成。从教材的前期策划和准备、单元设计、教学资源开发、编写团队、内容设置和编排到教学效果的评价和评估都有整体的体系构建，以满足教学大纲和课程目标的要求。本套教材不但注重培养学生听、说、读、写、译这些语言基本技能，而且强化学生思辨、创新能力的培养。

2. "学生为主体"＋"教师为主导"的"双主"教学理念

《指南》中提出大学英语教学应贯彻分类指导、因材施教的原则，以适应个性化教学的实际需要。新一轮的大学英语教学改革中也明确提出了"以教师为主导，以学生为主体"的"双主"教学理念。在教学过程中，教师的主导作用主要体现在课堂教学设计、教学组织、教学策略使用、教学管理和协调、课堂教学评价和评估等方面，而教师对课堂的主导方向要以满足学生的个性需求、促进学生的个性发展和自主学习为目的，只有两者相互结合，方能相得益彰，顺利实现大学英语教学改革目标。

3. "语言输入"＋"语言输出"的"双向"驱动教学体系

本套教材在课堂教学活动和课后练习中设计了很多"语言输入"和"语言输出"的互动环节，教材采用任务式、合作式、项目式、探究式等教学方法，体现以教师为主导、以学生为主体的教学理念，使教学活动满足从"语言输入"到"语言输出"的需求。课后练习的设计关注学生自主学习能力的培养，引导和帮助他们掌握学习策略，学会学习；促使学生从"被动学习"向"主动学习"转变，真正让学生成为学习过程中的主体，实现课内和课外学习"不断线"。

4. "平面教材"＋"立体化教材"的"双辅"交互优势

本套教材将大力推进最新信息技术与课程教学的融合，凸显现代学习方式的自主性、移动性、随时性等特点，发挥现代教育技术的推介作用。积极创建多元的教学与学习环境，利用互联网等信息基础设施和网络交流平台，使"平面教材"呈现出信息化教育的特征，形成"立体化教材"的特征。

此外，本套教材鼓励教师建设和使用微课、慕课，拓展教学内容，实施基于"教材平面内容"和"网上立体课件"的混合式教学模式，使学生朝着主动学习、自主学习和个性化学习方向发展，实现教学资源网络化、教学环境虚拟化、教学个性化、学习评估过程化等。

5. 以教材为引导、推动教师的自主专业发展，实现"教""学"相长

《纲要》明确指出，要"建设高素质教师队伍。提升教师素养，努力造就一支师德高尚，业务精湛，结构合理，充满活力的高素质专业化教师队伍"。教师的专业发展能力受多种主客观因素的影响，需要外在环境和管理机制的保障。教师专业发展的规律性特点可归纳为长期性、动态性、实践性和环境依托性。本套教材的编写和使用正是根据实践性和环境依托性的特点，编写和使用新教材的过程也是教师更新教学理念、提高教学技能的专业发展必经过程。

四、教材结构

本套教材共包含"读写"和"听说"两大系列。其中，"读写"系列分为初级、中级、高级三个级别，共六个分册。"听说"系列分为初级和中级两个级别，共四个分册。

在"读写"系列中，每册书有 8 个单元。每个单元分为 Section A 和 Section B 两部分。Section A 根据大学英语教学大纲的要求编制，包含一篇精读课文，课文后有生词表、短语和表达、缩略词、术语和课后练习。Section B 是按照专业英语学生的培养目标和要求编写，包含一篇与 Section A 同主题的阅读文章，旨在补充和强化专业阅读内容。两篇文章一易一难，每个单元都可以满足分级教学的需要和不同程度学生水平的需求，两个部分的练习形式多样，具有丰富性和系统性的特点。练习设计遵循语言学习的规律，针对不同层次、不同年级的学生，选材的难易程度、知识侧重点等方面均有所不同。

在"听说"系列中，每册书有 16 个单元，每个单元分为 Section A、Section B 及 Section C 三部分。其中，Section A 为听力技能训练，听力内容围绕 IT 相关主题展开。该部分由 Text A 和 Text B 两部分组成，前者针对 IT 及相关专业（非英语专业）学生，题目设计相对简单；后者针对英语专业（如科技英语）学生，题目设计难度有所增加。Section B 为口语技能训练，旨在培养学生的口头交际能力。Section C 为听力考试强化训练，该部分侧重应试，根据当下国内外几大英语考试（如大学英语四六级、托福、雅思等），全方位、多角度满足学生对英语学习的需求。希望通过题型多样、题量丰富的强化训练，让学生一方面熟悉并适应听力考试的多样题型，另一方面让学生检测自己的英语听力水平，提高自主学习能力。

五、教材特色

1. 素材原汁原味

本套教材的所有阅读和听力文本均选自英美国家真实的 IT 专业文本，包括 IT 相关专业的学术网站、期刊及英语原版教材。编者在选择文本时尽量选择新颖、有趣的分支话题，文章的语言也尽量避免过于严肃和刻板，使学生在理解和分析课文的过程中既能利用专业知识进行思考和判断，又不觉枯燥。

2. 内容注重实用性

本套教材的"读写"系列避免了国内同类教材培养目标单一、片面的缺陷，注重提高学生的多种技能。每个单元不仅包括阅读板块、翻译板块和写作板块，还针对 IT 及其相关专业的英语阅读、翻译、学术写作等技能进行系统的学习和训练。而在"听说"系列中，编者在选择听说文本的话题时，一方面迎合当今 IT 产业就业的发展趋势，另一方面也考虑与高校 IT 专业课程紧密相关，并参考国内各大重点高校 IT 专业设置，挑选出 IT 领域相关的热门话题，这些话题广泛涉及 IT 相关专业学生所关心的 IT 就业方面的问题、IT 专业知识的学习方法、全国重点高校 IT 相关专业课程中开设的典型编程语言、当今的网络环境、时下 IT 领域多项前沿技术等内容，以便在提升学生英语语言能力的同时了解和学习与 IT 相关的专业知识，突出语言运用，通过文本传递 IT 知识，重现真实 IT 场景。

3.　练习内容和形式丰富多样

本套教材在阅读和听力理解、语言知识学习及技能训练方面都设计了大量的练习，而且练习形式富于变化，如简答、判断、填空、选择、配对、翻译、图表、口语交际等，学生不仅可以学习词汇、短语等语言点，还可以提高阅读和听力理解能力、分析语言的能力及表达能力。

六、适用对象

本套教材特别适合计算机科学与技术、信息管理与信息系统、软件工程和网络工程等与 IT 相关专业的学生学习和使用，可以分阶段或分学期选用；也特别适合从事软件系统需求分析、设计、开发、测试、运行及维护工作的工程师和管理人员查阅和参考。编者在选材上保证与 IT 信息技术密切相关的同时，努力确保文章内容贴近生活，所选材料涵盖了当前教育、工作和社会领域的诸多热点，文字形象生动、可读性强。因此，本套教材也比较适合那些有一定英语基础，同时也喜爱计算机应用技术和互联网文化的人士阅读，以扩展知识，开拓视野。

七、编写团队

本套教材由大连外国语大学软件学院教师担任主编团队。参与编写的编者有来自全国各高校的大学英语教师、专业英语教师、计算机专业的教师、IT 职场的企业专家以及旅居海外的专家和学者。

本套教材在编写过程中得到校企合作教材编写组的大力支持，在此表示衷心感谢。校企合作编写组成员包括李鸿飞、王文智、姜超、韩参、蒋振彬、梁浩、刘志强（排名不分先后）。

本套教材在编写过程中也得到了大连外国语大学软件学院的领导与英语教研室所有老师的鼎力支持，在此表示感谢。

由于编者水平有限，错误与缺点在所难免，恳请读者批评指正。

司炳月

2017 年 6 月

Contents

Contents

Unit 1
Learning Computer Science by Going to College

Learning Objectives

- To learn several ways of studying information science
- To learn to grasp the main idea of a paragraph
- To learn to introduce yourself

Section A Listening

 *

Pre-Listening

Direction: Work in pairs and discuss the following questions.

1. What is your major? Are you familiar with your major?

2. Do you think computer science is a popular major in college?

Warm-up Activities

⚙ Vocabulary

relatively	['relətɪvlɪ]	*adv.*	by comparison to something else 相对地；比较地
reveal	[rɪ'vil]	*vt.*	allow or cause to be seen 显示；透露；揭露；泄露
curriculum	[kə'rɪkjələm]	*n.*	subjects included in a course of study or taught at a particular school, college 课程
gender	['dʒɛndə]	*n.*	the properties that distinguish organisms on the basis of their reproductive roles 性；性别
confer	[kən'fɜ]	*vt.*	present 授予；给予
Israel	['ɪzrɪəl]	*n.*	以色列（亚洲国家）；犹太人，以色列人
Malaysia	[mə'leʒə]	*n.*	马来西亚；马来群岛
Guyana	[gaɪ'ænə]	*n.*	圭亚那（拉丁美洲国家）

❶ Activity One

Direction: In this section, you will hear a news report. After listening, you should choose the best answer to each question. Now listen to the news report.

1. What is the news report mainly about?

   A. Computer science is widely taught in most schools and universities.

   B. Computer science is not extensively taught in colleges.

---

* 请扫描二维码下载全书的音频及课件资源。

C. Computer science is extensively taught in colleges.

D. Computer science is not a required course in most countries.

2. In 2014, how many high schools opened the subject of computer science in America?

   A. 14%.   **B.** 50%.

   C. 10%.   **D.** 20%.

3. Which country's curriculum does **NOT** include computer science according to the passage?

   A. New Zealand.   **B.** Israel.

   C. South Korea.   **D.** Japan.

② Activity Two

Direction: Listen to another news report and choose the best answer to each question.

4. What is the news report mainly about?

   A. The significance of computer science education.

   B. The computer science education in Western countries.

   C. The issue of gender gap in computer science education.

   D. The number of people who get computer science education.

5. How many computer science degrees were conferred to women in 2012 in America?

   A. 12%.   **B.** 20%.

   C. 54%.   **D.** 50%.

6. Which country's women made up 54% of computer science graduates?

   A. The U.S.A.   **B.** Malaysia.

   C. Guyana.   **D.** China.

While-Listening

Text A How to Write Codes

⚙ Vocabulary

path	[pæθ]	*n.*	way or method 途径；方法
vocational	[voˈkeʃənl]	*adj.*	especially providing or undergoing training in special skills 职业的，行业的
intermingle	[ˌɪntəˈmɪŋgl]	*vt.*	combine things into one 使混合
constraint	[kənˈstrent]	*n.*	something that limits one's freedom of action 约束；限制；强制

① Activity One

Direction: In this section, you will hear a long conversation. After listening, you should choose the best answer to each question. Now listen to the conversation.

1. What is the conversation mainly about?

   A. The traditional way of learning how to write codes.

   B. The effective way of learning how to write codes.

   C. The different ways of learning how to write codes.

   D. The similar way of learning how to write codes.

2. How many paths are there (for students) to learn how to write codes?

   A. One.   **B.** Two.

   C. Three.   **D.** Four.

3. According to the conversation, when do students attend vocational schools?

   A. At night.   **B.** During term time.

   C. On weekends.   **D.** On holidays.

4. Which is the most basic step for students to learn how to write codes?

   A. Going to colleges.   **B.** Going to vocational schools.

   C. By self-study.   **D.** None of the above.

5. Which is the most essential process of learning how to write codes?

    A. Going to colleges.   **B.** Going to vocational schools.

    C. By self-study.   **D.** None of the above.

② Activity Two

Direction: Listen again and decide whether the following statements are true (T) or false (F).

6. The professor thinks Steven has asked a simple question. (   )

7. The traditional way of learning how to write codes is to learn basic knowledge about programming languages. (   )

8. In the professor's opinion, people can just enroll in regular school to continue their study or learn practical skills. (   )

9. All these ways are viable and single, and they have their own strengths and weaknesses. (   )

10. In the professor's opinion, the best way to learn how to write codes is to study by oneself. (   )

Text B Learning Computer Science by Going to College

⚙ Vocabulary

decent	['disnt]	*adj.*	socially or conventionally correct; refined or virtuous 正派的；得体的；相当好的
vacancy	['veikənsi]	*n.*	being unoccupied 空缺；空位
take into account			考虑；重视；体谅
prevailing	[prɪ'velɪŋ]	*adj.*	encountered generally especially at the present time 流行的
mindset	['maɪndset]	*n.*	a habitual or characteristic mental attitude that determines how you will interpret and respond to situations 心态；倾向
conference	['kɑnfərəns]	*n.*	a prearranged meeting for consultation or exchange of information or discussion (especially one with a formal agenda) 会议；讨论

❶ Activity One

*Direction: In this section, you will hear a talk **ONLY ONCE**. While listening, you may write **NO MORE THAN THREE WORDS** for each gap. Make sure the word(s) you fill in is (are) both grammatically and semantically acceptable. Now listen to the talk.*

Learning Computer Science by Going to College

I. Advantages

A. Numerous companies only hire people who have **1.** _____.

Some companies demand employees must graduate from universities like Princeton, Cornell or **2.** _____.

Many companies do not take into account employees' **3.** _____ and skills.

Getting education in colleges may offer students more **4.** _____ that self-taught people may not get.

B. Colleges provide students with a **5.** _____.

Universities help students make a **6.** _____ with famous companies and provide them with resources that students might not have access to on their own.

II. Disadvantages

A. The most obvious one — **7.** _____.

College education is really expensive, especially for some popular majors such as **8.** _____.

Living on campus is expensive.

Renting your own **9.** _____ also costs a lot.

B. The second drawback is time.

College takes a **10.** _____ of four years.

Some activities in school will not directly benefit students.

❷ Activity Two

Direction: Listen again and decide whether the following statements are true (T) or false (F).

11. Companies tend to label people into two categories: degree or non-degree. (   )

12. In the speaker's opinion, some companies are pretty short-sighted. (   )

13. Nowadays, many schools may offer internships for their students, or some companies even recruit directly from schools. (   )

14. All the activities and time in school will directly benefit students. (   )

Post-Listening

Direction: Work in pairs and discuss the following questions.

1. Have you ever enrolled in a vocational school?

2. Do you think "self-study" is necessary? Why or why not?

Section B Speaking

Speaking to Introduce Yourself

"Tell us about yourself" is a question often asked in a work situation by HR managers or project directors, or in any social situation where information about you may be needed or helpful. Introducing yourself is far more than just saying your name. It composes part of the first impression you make on people, and it is a way of making new connections with those you newly come across either in work or life.

Introducing yourself to strangers can be tricky because what you say largely depends on the occasion and the audience. This means that you may introduce yourself quite differently depending on whether you are having a job interview, or meeting with a new work mate in office, or giving a speech at a conference, or just starting a conversation with someone at a party. Therefore, it is important to be prepared for the occasion, just as you need to be prepared for a job interview, and to have some knowledge of your audience beforehand.

Knowing the occasion and the audience, you are in a much better position to introduce yourself appropriately, effectively and interestingly so that people will respond to your self-introduction favorably. The following are some tips to help you prepare your self-introduction.

- Get to know the audience and the situation and decide what information about you is wanted or would be meaningful for the occasion and the audience.

- Start your self-introduction by greeting the audience (like "Good morning!" or "Hello,

everyone!") and stating your name clearly. In a formal or professional situation, it is important to state your full name.

- Give a one-sentence description of what you do or study professionally. State who you are, who you work with, and what you do briefly as in "I am an information engineer working with the World Bank on information security".

- Choose one focus for your self-introduction and support it by relevant information. Do not run into a lengthy narration of life story or try to cover everything about you in a 2-minute self-introduction; instead, focus on the thing that would be most appropriate and meaningful to the situation and the audience. For example, in a job interview, it would be appropriate and effective to focus on your education, experience or personal traits that are related to the job you are seeking.

- Keep good timing. Usually a self-introduction may last 1 to 3 minutes depending on the situation. Don't launch into a ten-minute story about your education background or career path.

- Communicate effectively by means of keeping eye contact and keeping your voice clear and loud enough for everyone to hear.

- Be confident and friendly. While speaking, remember to keep your body erect and straight. You can also smile and use gesture properly to convey a confident and friendly impression.

Questions to Think About

1. Think about the focus of your self-introduction when you are to introduce yourself to 1) a group of new office mates, 2) some new friends at karaoke and 3) your project leader. What different focus will you choose?

2. Before a job interview, why is it important to get to know the company/organization? Why is it important to get to know the responsibilities of the post you are applying for?

3. Preparing a self-introduction is actually a way of truly getting to know yourself and discovering your meaningful connection with the world. While starting your career in IT, how would you define the connection between yourself and the career you choose?

Communication Tasks

1. When you are about to start your career, what do you think would be your dream job or dream post? Discuss with your classmates and tell them why you like the job.

2. What qualifications and experiences would qualify you for your dream job? Make a list of your strengths that will make you a qualified or competitive applicant for the job.

3. Based on the list of information in the previous task, prepare a 2-minute speech of self-introduction. Present the speech to your classmates as if you are introducing yourself in a job interview.

Section C Exam Spotlight

1 Activity One

*Direction: In this section, you will hear three news reports **ONLY ONCE**. At the end of each news report, you will be given 10 seconds to answer the questions.*

News Item One

1. **A.** It is a special day in America.

   B. It is on the third Sunday in June.

   C. It celebrates the importance of fathers.

   D. It is time for people to thank father figures.

2. **A.** It is a common father expression in English.

   B. It originates from William Blake's poem.

   C. It means a boy is very much like his father.

   D. It means people's personalities form early.

News Item Two

3. **A.** A 17-year-old girl.   **B.** A 15-year-old boy.

   C. A 23-year-old woman.   **D.** An 18-year-old man.

4. **A.** One month later.   **B.** Two months later.

   C. Immediately.   **D.** Two weeks later.

News Item Three

5. **A.** All.　　　　　　　　　**B.** Some.

   C. One.　　　　　　　　　**D.** None.

6. **A.** Hong Kong and Taiwan.　　**B.** Taiwan and Tokyo.

   C. Tokyo and Seoul.　　　　　**D.** Hong Kong and Seoul.

② Activity Two

Direction: In this section, you will hear a conversation between two students. After listening, you are required to fill in the blanks with the exact words you have just heard.

Boy: 7. _____ I just finished the story I was working on for our creative writing course.

Girl: I haven't quite finished mine yet. 8. _____.

Boy: How come?

Girl: Well, I was really happy to be writing 9. _____. But after the first new pages, 10. _____. I just couldn't write any more.

Boy: The same thing happened to me. I thought it meant I lack imagination.

Girl: Well, Mrs. Wilson said 11. _____ for writers to get stuck like that.

Boy: You went to talk to her about it?

Girl: Actually, I want to ask for more time to finish the assignment. But instead she gave me some advice about 12. _____.
She said that the first thing I should do is to write anything that comes into my head even if it doesn't make any sense, sort of a warm-up exercise.

Boy: That is interesting. When I get stuck, I shift to something else, you know, do some work for one of my other courses.

Girl: Well, her methods seem to have worked for me. I've written most of the story, and I should be able to 13. _____. But first I need to go to the jewelry store.

Boy: You are going shopping? Can't you wait until you finish your story?

Girl: I am going there for my story. 14. _____.
So I want to take a look at how the jewelry cases are arranged, where the security cameras are located, that sort of thing.

❸ Activity Three

Direction: In this section, you will hear two long conversations. At the end of each conversation, you will be given 15 seconds to answer the questions.

Conversation One

15. **A.** Very good.　　　　　　　　　**B.** Interesting.

　　C. Too specialized.　　　　　　　**D.** Too general.

16. **A.** Logic.　　　　　　　　　　　　**B.** Writing.

　　C. History.　　　　　　　　　　　**D.** Mathematics.

17. **A.** The man chose Professor White's course once.

　　B. The woman is in favor of Professor White.

　　C. Professor White's course is welcomed by the students.

　　D. The man won't choose Professor White's course any more.

Conversation Two

18. **A.** The bowling style.　　　　　　　**B.** The rugby style.

　　B. The basketball style.　　　　　　**D.** The NBA style.

19. **A.** Southern Europe.　　　　　　　**B.** Northern Europe.

　　C. Russia.　　　　　　　　　　　　**D.** Latin America.

20. **A.** To make sure that the letter is "T" instead of "D".

　　B. To tell the physician he needs a table.

　　C. To indicate the physician is like a table.

　　D. To make fun of the physician.

❹ Activity Four

Direction: In this section, you will hear a passage THREE TIMES. When the passage is read for the first time, you should listen carefully for its general idea. When the passage is read for the second time, you are required to fill in the blanks with the exact words you have just heard. Finally, when the passage is read for the third time, you should check what you have written.

Extinction is a difficult concept to grasp. It is an **21.** _____ concept. It is not at all like the killing of individual life forms that can be renewed through normal processes of reproduction. Nor is it simply **22.** _____ numbers. Nor is it damage that can somehow be remedied or for which some substitute can be found. Nor is it something that only affects our own generation. Nor is it something that could be remedied by some supernatural power. It is, rather an **23.** _____ and final act for which there is no remedy on Earth or in heaven. A species once extinct, it's gone forever. However many generations **24.** _____ us in coming centuries, none of them will ever see this species that we extinguish. Not only are we bringing about the extinction of life **25.** _____, we are also making the land and the air and the sea so toxic that the very conditions of life are being destroyed. **26.** _____ basic natural resources , not only are the nonrenewable resources being **27.** _____ in a frenzy of processing, consuming and **28.** _____ , but we are also ruining much of our renewable resources, such as the very soil itself on which terrestrial life depends. The change that is taking place on the Earth and in our minds is one of the greatest changes ever to take place in human affairs, perhaps the greatest, since what we are talking about is not simply another historical change or cultural **29.** _____ , but a change of geological and biological as well as psychological order of **30.** _____ .

Unit 2
IT Career and Corporate Culture

- **Learning Objectives**

  - To learn basic information of several IT fields
  - To learn to listen to details of a passage
  - To learn to speak to compete

Section **A** Listening

Pre-Listening

Direction: Work in pairs and discuss the following questions.

1. How many IT career paths do you know? What are they?

2. Why did you choose IT as your major? What job do you want to do in the future?

Warm-up Activities

⚙ Vocabulary

undergraduate	[ˌʌndəˈgrædʒuət]	*n.*	a university student who has not yet received a first degree 大学生
rigorous	[ˈrɪgərəs]	*adj.*	rigidly accurate; allowing no deviation from a standard 严格的，严厉的；严密的；严酷的
unequivocal	[ˌʌnɪˈkwɪvəkl]	*adj.*	admitting of no doubt or misunderstanding 明确的；不含糊的
gauge	[geɪdʒ]	*vt.*	make a judgement about (something) 判断（某事物）

❶ Activity One

Direction: In this section, you will hear an article. After listening, you should choose the best answer to each question. Now listen to the article.

1. What is the main idea of the article?

    A. IT roles require certifications.

    B. Rigorous programs can take years of hard work to complete.

    C. There are ample opportunities to pursue a successful career in IT education.

    D. IT industry is far-reaching and changing rapidly.

2. According to the article, what is a superb career path?

   A. IT engineer.　　　　　　　　　**B.** IT education.

   C. IT manager.　　　　　　　　　**D.** IT technician.

3. Which is **WRONG** about universities?

   A. Universities offer excellent programs in computer science.

   B. Universities offer excellent programs in systems analysis.

   C. Universities offer programs in some other aspects of IT.

   D. Universities can keep up with changing technology.

② Activity Two

Direction: Listen to another article and decide whether the following statements are true (T) or false (F).

4. I'm often asked if IT is still a good career choice. My answer is an absolutely yes. (　　)

5. Adding to this excitement is the never change we experience in this market. (　　)

6. This year everyone wants Big Data specialists in IT industry. (　　)

While-Listening

Text A Field Services and Cyber Services

⚙ Vocabulary

bedrock	['bɛdrɑk]	*n.*	the basic ideas, features or facts on which something is based 基础
validate	['vælɪdet]	*vt.*	show or confirm the validity of something 证实；验证
military	['mɪlətɛrɪ]	*n.*	the forces of a nation 军队；军人
troubleshoot	['trʌblʃut]	*vt.*	solve problems 故障排解

🅐 Activity One

Direction: In this section, you will hear the first part of a passage. After listening, you should choose the best answer to each question. Now listen to the passage.

1. What is the bedrock of IT?

    A. Service and support.　　　　　　**B.** Technology.

    C. IT technicians.　　　　　　　　**D.** Break-fix support.

2. Which is **NOT** involved in the cloud itself?

    A. Physical infrastructure.　　　　**B.** Mobile access.

    C. End users require touch.　　　　**D.** IT devices.

3. Many tech schools and universities offer all of the following except _____.

    A. programs that provide basic background in hardware and software

    B. programs that provide basic background in networking

    C. security-certifications

    D. certificates from CompTIA

4. To get start, which one will you at least want from CompTIA?

    A. Network+.　　　　　　　　　　**B.** Security+.

    C. A+ certification.　　　　　　　**D.** All of the above.

5. What is the main topic of the passage?

    A. IT certificates.　　　　　　　　**B.** Basic contents in field service.

    C. IT devices.　　　　　　　　　　**D.** Influence of IT.

🅑 Activity Two

Direction: Listen to the rest of the passage and decide whether the following statements are true (T) or false (F).

6. Cyber security arguably requires less expertise than field service. (　　)

7. Every business needs cyber security or some form of network or data security. (　　)

8. It is absolutely necessary for the degree to be in the field of security. (　　)

9. Cyber security typically requires inside-the-box thinking skills. (   )

10. One place to start is with both CompTIA's Security+ certification and software providers. (   )

Text B Combine IT Expertise with Knowledge of a Specific Industry

⚙ Vocabulary

| vertical | ['vɜːtɪkl] | *adj.* | being oriented vertically 垂直的，直立的 |
| consultant | [kən'sʌltənt] | *n.* | an expert who gives advice 顾问 |

① Activity One

*Direction: In this section, you will hear the first part of a passage **ONLY ONCE**. While listening, you may write **NO MORE THAN THREE WORDS** for each gap. Make sure the word(s) you fill in is (are) both grammatically and semantically acceptable. Now listen to the passage.*

Business Consulting/Vertical Industries/Professional Services

One of the best things you can do with IT expertise is combine it with knowledge of a **1.** _____ industry. Of course, that requires additional knowledge, experience, or both. But few business workers have **2.** _____ of both IT and their industry. The person who comprehends both is invaluable.

A business consultant or technology professional services consultant with IT expertise has **3.** _____. Those options could lie within the IT department or within a line of business inside the enterprise. He or she could work as a provider of **4.** _____ or as a business consultant independently or as a part of a service organization. There are many channels in the market requiring these skills from solution architects with a **5.** _____ (VAR) to a technology consultant or business consultant working as part of an IT channel partner, VAR or even a traditional consulting firm. This is a high-growth, **6.** _____ with many routes to service markets as a professional in business and IT combined.

There are several high-growth industries in which IT is increasingly important. These include **7.** _____ , **8.** _____ , energy and **9.** _____ (or evolving areas such as service provider, or SP). For example, healthcare facilities increasingly depend on interconnected equipment and data (such as Internet of Things, or IoT). Any IT expert who also understands the unique needs of healthcare or a given vertical will be in high demand. Lastly, the topic and technologies within IoT for almost any vertical is an area with **10.** _____. IoT itself will have a very positive impact on careers in each of the topics covered today. We'll expand on this topic more in the future with opinions and projections from industry experts and use cases for you to consider as a potential next step in your IT career.

② Activity Two

Direction: Listen to the rest of the passage and decide whether the following statements are true (T) or false (F).

11. Anyone can be an IT management if he has made great efforts before. (   )

12. Everyone in an IT career will have to decide whether to continue with a technical focus or shift into a managerial role. (   )

13. One place to start is to learn different kinds of programming languages. (   )

14. At companies with more than 1,000 employees, it's not unusual for one or two managers to oversee the entire IT function. (   )

15. You'll need deep knowledge of not only technology but also business. (   )

Post-Listening

Direction: Work in pairs and discuss the following questions.

1. Are you suitable for jobs in the field of IT? Why or why not?

2. Which IT career path do you like most? Why?

Section B Speaking

Speaking to Compete and Win

Since the 1990s, various English-speaking contests are organized all over China at various levels in order to encourage students to speak better English. Many students value the experience of competing in an English-speaking contest as a big event in their college life. Universities are also making greater efforts in order to win in these contests.

In most English-speaking contests, there will be a prepared speech based on a given topic, a wide range of topics for impromptu speeches and a Q&A session when contestants answer questions raised by question masters. To win a public speaking contest in English is very difficult, but it is worthwhile to try, for the experience alone will greatly benefit your English and your personality.

In preparing the prepared speech, the following tips may be of help to you:

Decide on a point you feel strongly about. You can expect the topic of the prepared speech to be very broad. It is advisable that you narrow the topic down to a more manageable perspective that you know or feel or care deeply about. Such a perspective will ensure you to have something to say from the bottom of your heart. Thus your speech can be personal, passionate, convincing and impactful. Meanwhile, you should know to avoid politically sensitive content and explosive issues so as not to cause any feelings of discomfort on the audience's part. Be careful with jokes and humor. Make sure they are dignified and "safe" for the occasion.

State your point clearly in a powerful statement. This statement is the purpose statement of your speech and it is to be restated and echoed throughout the speech, supported by evidence and other details. Only by doing so can your speech achieve unity and coherence.

Use a variety of support. No matter how much you know about the topic, your knowledge may still prove inadequate for a convincing speech. To use resources and do research work is a must in preparing a speech. The resources you can use include books, newspapers, magazines, and the Internet. Research work will lead you to a variety of supporting material that may be of your service—stories, reports, examples, statistics, metaphors, images, quotations, etc.

Use a simple structure. The wisdom and beauty of your speech should be conveyed mostly through content and language, while the structure can remain straightforward. The "point—support—summary" form will work fine for most speeches. A tricky or loose structure may easily lead audience to confusion.

Polish your language. Get whatever can help you to improve the English in your script. It is suggested that you use shorter words and plain English to highlight the content and rhythm of your speech. Replace words that are difficult to pronounce with simpler, brisker ones. Also avoid lengthy, tricky quotes that are difficult to understand.

Practice your delivery. Prepared speech is the only part of a contest over which you have total control. So spare no efforts to practice delivering it. Ask your teachers and fellow students to be your audience and judges. Listen to their feedback and suggestions until you achieve "studied naturalness".

The impromptu speech and the Q&A session are quite different. In major speech contests, you get to choose the topic for your impromptu speech 15 to 20 minutes before you go on the stage, which means you have 15 to 20 minutes to prepare. The Q&A session directly follows your impromptu speech. You need to answer the questions with no time to think or prepare. The topics for impromptu speeches may range from personal to cultural, campus issues to current affairs. The impromptu speech is the most challenging part of a speech contest because you get the topic "out of the blue", and you need to be able to stay calm and think on your own. In planning your impromptu speech, follow the simple steps below and you'll find the task much more manageable.

Make sure you understand the topic. It is essential that you understand the topic and the question. If you come across a new word, look it up. Spend a minute to digest the topic.

Develop a clear central point. You just let yourself respond naturally to the topic and settle on one major point or stand. Jot down a few key words, a turn of phrase, or a neat statement to express your point. Keep this point in your mind. Your speech is going to evolve around this point and this statement.

Work out an outline. Determine two or three sub points surrounding your central point and search your mind for necessary supporting details. Keep the idea clear and logical by using markers such as "first", "next", "finally", etc. These markers identify each point and help the audience keep track of your thoughts. In your outline, you only need to jot down a few key words or phrases to indicate the points and support, and let yourself see the organization. There's no need to prepare a script.

Have an effective beginning and ending. Maybe you can not completely avoid rambling or faltering in the middle of the speech, but make sure that you have very neat, effective beginning and ending. In the beginning, let the audience know what you are going to say; in the ending, bring the audience back to you point by restating your point in a stronger note.

Look confident. Try to look calm and confident regardless of how nervous you might feel. Keep a reasonable pace; do not speak too fast or use too many vocalized pauses. Maintain your composure and talk in an assured manner, and you will make a good impression on the audience and the judges.

Winning or losing is not just about the few minutes on the stage. It is more about the accumulation of knowledge and experience that is key to making a competent speaker. It is also about the person that you are. The winners are the ones who are confident in the person that they are, and they can let their personality shine through their speeches on the stage.

Questions to Think About

1. Do you think an impromptu speech is fundamentally different from a prepared speech? Why or why not?

2. If you are given the topic "My Other Self" for a prepared speech, what perspective will you have a strong feeling to deliver the speech?

3. Why is it advisable to use markers such as "firstly", "lastly", etc. when giving an impromptu speech?

4. If you need to polish your language in the prepared speech, what should be your strategy concerning language use in the impromptu speech?

Communication Tasks

1. Compose a 400-word speech based on one of the following corporate slogans. Your speech should be an extensive interpretation of this slogan.

   (1) Just do it. (Nike)

   (2) When there is no tomorrow. (Fedex)

   (3) Pleasure is the path to joy. (Haagen-Dazs)

2. Have you ever had any doubts about a company slogan, or about the corporate culture of a company or an organization? Why do you have issues with it? What are your doubts? Explore the meaning and influence of the slogan or corporate culture and give a 3-minute speech explaining your doubts or points of disagreement.

3. The following are some impromptu speech topics. Choose one and give yourself 15 minutes to try to work out an outline for the speech.

   Quotes:

   (1) Man does not only want to be rich; he wants to be richer than others.

   (2) Corporate culture is simply a shared way of doing something with a passion.

   (3) If we have a culture where we are incredibly self-critical, we don't get comfortable with our success.

   Topical issues:

   (4) Why do you think competitive talent shows like *American Idol* and *Voice of China* have attracted so many people?

(5) According to a survey done in Zhejiang Province earlier in 2016, 94% of social media users in China have received requests from their relatives or acquaintances to cast a vote online for their children in various contests ranging from "cutest baby" to dancing. In most cases, the receiver of the request has not heard from the sender for a long time, nor does he know the children involved. What do you think of this phenomenon?

Section C Exam Spotlight

❶ Activity One

*Direction: In this section, you will hear three news reports **ONLY ONCE**. At the end of each news report, you will be given 10 seconds to answer the questions.*

News Item One

1. **A.** In the temple.　　　　　　　　　**B.** In the city center.

   C. In the bus.　　　　　　　　　　**D.** Outside the hospital.

2. **A.** Worshipers of Shiite Muslim.　　　**B.** Worshipers of Sunni Muslim.

   C. Militants of Shiite Muslim.　　　　**D.** Militants of Sunni Muslim.

News Item Two

3. **A.** Drug abuse.　　　　　　　　　　**B.** Sexual abuse.

   C. Alcoholism.　　　　　　　　　　**D.** Corruption.

4. **A.** Six boys who lived in Phnom Penh slum testified against Walker.

   B. The Japanese teacher was sentenced to 10 years in prison.

   C. The judge ordered Walker to pay $5,000 to each of the six boys.

   D. The teacher was sentenced to 10 years in jail by an Australian court.

News Item Three

5. **A.** She thought it was correct.　　　　**B.** She thought it was incomplete.

   C. She thought it was not true.　　　　**D.** She thought it was complete.

6. **A.** 140.   **B.** 14.

    C. 410.   **D.** 1,400.

② Activity Two

Direction: In this section, you will listen to a teacher talking in a biology class. After listening, you are required to fill in the blanks with the exact words you have just heard.

Bees are **7.** _____ that are found all over the world. There are over **8.** _____ different species of bees, but only **9.** _____ of these occur in North America.

Bees can be divided into two groups according to **10.** _____. Solitary bees live alone. On the other hand, social bees, like ants, live in groups. Only about six hundred species are of this social category.

11. _____ are interesting because in their "society" there are different classes of bees. Each class **12.** _____. Queen bees **13.** _____. Workers are underdeveloped females. They work in the hive but never reproduce. Males do not work; their only task is to mate with the queen.

14. _____ occur as males and females. Every female makes a nest in the ground where she will lay her eggs. The nest consists of many cells. After an egg is laid and put in a cell, the female also adds some **15.** _____ for food. Then she **16.** _____. The female then goes elsewhere. When the eggs hatch, the larvae will **17.** _____ which the female left for them.

③ Activity Three

Direction: In this section, you will hear two long conversations. At the end of each conversation, you will be given 15 seconds to answer the questions.

Conversation One

18. **A.** He was very sick and was taken to the hospital.

    B. He fell and hurt himself badly.

    C. He broke his leg in a traffic accident.

    D. He was working when something suddenly fell onto his head.

19. **A.** Better.   **B.** Never too well yet.

   C. Much better.   **D.** Even worse.

20. **A.** His leg is broken and his ribs hurt very much.

   B. He has a chest pain and can hardly breathe.

   C. He can hardly remember anything that has happened.

   D. He feels too weak to talk.

Conversation Two

21. **A.** Relaxing.   **B.** Watching TV.

   C. Knitting sacks.   **D.** Collecting buttons.

22. **A.** She thinks it is very helpful.

   B. She thinks it is a waste of time.

   C. She thinks it is very interesting.

   D. She thinks the man can learn a lot from it.

23. **A.** Have a rest.   **B.** Have a good time.

   C. Have a bath.   **D.** Have an exercise.

④ Activity Four

*Direction: In this section, you will hear a passage **THREE TIMES**. When the passage is read for the first time, you should listen carefully for its general idea. When the passage is read for the second time, you are required to fill in the blanks with the exact words you have just heard. Finally, when the passage is read for the third time, you should check what you have written.*

   Graphics are used in textbooks as part of the language of the discipline, as in math or economics, or as study aids. Authors use graphic aids to **24.** _____ and expand on concepts taken up in the text because graphics are yet another way of portraying relationships and **25.** _____ connections.

   Graphics are used extensively in natural sciences and social sciences. Social scientists work with statistics **26.** _____ data, and the best way to present these statistics is often in graphic form. Graphics are included not merely as a means of making the information easier for the student to grasp, but as an integral part of the way social scientists think. Many textbooks,

27. _____ those in economics, contain appendixes that provide specific information on reading and working with graphic material.

Make it a practice to **28.** _____ attentively the titles, captions, headings, and other material connected with the graphics. These elements **29.** _____ and usually explain what you are looking at. When you are examining graphics, the **30.** _____ questions to ask are (a.)What is this item about? and (b.)What key idea is the author **31.** _____ ?

One warning: Unless you integrate your reading of graphics with the text, you may make a wrong assumption. **32.** _____ , from a chart indicating that 33 percent of firstborn children in a research sample did not feel close to their fathers, you might assume that some dreadful influence was at work on the firstborn children. However, a careful reading of the text **33.** _____ that most of the firstborn children in the sample were from single-parent homes in which the father was absent.

Unit 3

Coding: The Essential Step to Be a Professional IT Engineer

Learning Objectives

- To learn basic knowledge about programming language
- To learn to exclude useless information
- To learn expressions of welcoming and greeting

Section Ⓐ Listening

Pre-Listening

Direction: Work in pairs and discuss the following questions.

1. What do you know about programming languages?

2. Do you want to study programming languages? Why or why not?

Warm-up Activities

⚙ Vocabulary

recipient	[rɪˈsɪpɪənt]	*n.*	a person who gets something 接受者
societal	[səˈsaɪətl]	*adj.*	relating to human society and its members 社会的
aptitude	[ˈæptɪˌtud]	*n.*	inherent ability 天资；自然倾向

① Activity One

Direction: In this section, you will hear a news report. After listening, you should choose the best answer to each question. Now listen to the news report.

1. When did Reshma Saujani found the organization called "Girls Who Code"?

    A. In 2010. **B.** In 2011.

    C. In 2001. **D.** In 2012.

2. Which one is **NOT** included in STEM?

    A. Society. **B.** Technology.

    C. Engineering. **D.** Mathematics.

② Activity Two

Direction: Listen again and decide whether the following statements are true (T) or false (F).

3. American colleges and universities awarded about 1,700,000 bachelor's degrees in the school year ending in 2010. (   )

4. Fifty-seven percent of the women earned degrees in computer and information sciences. (   )

5. The under-representation of women in the fields of STEM is caused by an aptitude issue. (   )

6. Google was the first business to invest in "Girls Who Code". (   )

While-Listening

Text A Teaching Kids About Computers

⚙ Vocabulary

syntax	['sɪntæks]	*n.*	the grammatical arrangement of words in sentences 句法
algorithm	['ælgə'rɪðəm]	*n.*	a precise rule (or set of rules) specifying how to solve some problem [计][数] 算法；运算法则
protocol	['protə'kɔl]	*n.*	(computer science) rules determining the format and transmission of data （计算机数据传递的）协议
paradigm	['pærə'daɪm]	*n.*	type of sth.; pattern 范例；样式
abstraction	[æb'strækʃən]	*n.*	a concept or idea not associated with any specific instance 抽象；抽象概念
combustion	[kəm'bʌstʃən]	*n.*	a process in which a substance reacts with oxygen to give heat and light 燃烧；氧化
Snow Leopard		*n.*	苹果公司 2009 年发布的 Mac OSX 操作系统的一个版本
CPU (Central Processing Unit)			中央处理器

RAM (Random-Access Memory)   随机存取存储器

ROM (Read Only Memory)   只读存储器

---

① Activity One

Direction: In this section, you will hear the first part of a speech. After listening, you should choose the best answer to each question. Now listen to the speech.

1. What is the main idea of the beginning part?

   A. Computer science is an esoteric, weird science discipline.

   B. Little girls can ask amazing questions.

   C. Little girls don't know that they are not supposed to like computers. It's the parents who do.

   D. Parents do have problems to understand computer science.

2. What is **NOT** mentioned about programming?

   A. Syntax and controls.   **B.** Data structures.

   C. Algorithms and practices.   **D.** Numbers.

3. Which one is **WRONG** about computers?

   A. They are smaller and smaller.   **B.** We can see clearly how they work.

   C. We cannot talk to them.   **D.** Parents don't tell us how they work.

4. What do parents always do?

   A. They teach their kids how the computer works.

   B. They answer kids' questions about computer cautiously.

   C. They tell kids they cannot be astronauts.

   D. They cannot answer kids' questions about computer properly.

5. Which one is **CORRECT** according to the passage?

   A. Computer science is magic.

   B. Computer science is complicated.

   C. Computer science just happens so fast.

   D. None of the above.

❷ Activity Two

Direction: Listen to the rest of the speech and decide whether the following statements are true (T) or false (F).

6. Unless we give kids tools to build with computers, we are raising only consumers instead of creators. (   )

7. In order to teach kids to learn to code, the author wrote a book in which all the characters are parts of the computer or the computer science. (   )

8. Ruby is completely fearless, imaginative, but she can be inconfident sometimes. (   )

9. According to the author, Linux is really efficient and easy to understand. (   )

10. We can learn about CPU, RAM and ROM when we build a computer together. (   )

Text B Dynamic Programming Language and Statically Typed Languages

⚙ Vocabulary

debug   [diˈbʌg]   *vt.*   locate and correct errors in a computer program code 调试；除错

❶ Activity One

*Direction: In this section, you will hear a passage about the dynamic programming language Java. You will hear the passage **ONLY ONCE**. While listening, you may fill in the blanks with the exact words you have just heard. Make sure the word(s) you fill in is (are) both grammatically and semantically acceptable. Now listen to the passage.*

Dynamic Programming Language

Not to be **1.** _____ with Java, JavaScript is a primarily **2.** _____ scripting language used for front-end development. JavaScript is compatible across all **3.** _____ and is used to create interactive web apps, often through libraries such as jQuery and front-end frameworks such as AngularJS, Ember.js, React, and more.

JavaScript can now also be used as a **4.** _____ language through the Node.js platform, and while Node.js is relatively new, the community is gaining a lot of **5.** _____. You can also build **6.** _____ mobile apps with JavaScript through using **7.** _____ such as phonegap, while Facebook's React Native aims to allow you to build native mobile apps with JavaScript.

However, JavaScript is also known to be a difficult language as it is **8.** _____ and thus is difficult to debug. There are statically typed versions such as Microsoft's Type Script or the JSX that React uses.

❷ Activity Two

*Direction: In this section, you will hear a passage about the statically typed languages. You will hear the passage **ONLY ONCE**. While listening, you may match the following five items with four programming languages marked A, B, C and D. Now listen to the passage.*

A. Java   **B.** C   **C.** C++   **D.** C #

9. It is often used to program system software. (   )

10. It is a general-purpose language and 90 percent of Fortune 500 companies use it. (   )

11. It takes complex code to perform simple tasks. (   )

12. It runs primarily on Microsoft Windows. (   )

13. Facebook has developed several high performance and high reliability components with it. (   )

Post-Listening

Direction: Work in pairs and discuss the following questions.

1. Do you want to be a professional IT engineer? Why or why not?

2. How many essential qualities do you think a professional IT engineer should have?

Section B Speaking

Welcoming and Greeting

A welcome speech, as a formal gesture of hospitality, is a public greeting to a visitor or a guest, or a group of visitors or participants, to make them feel welcome, appreciated and at home. A welcome speech may be of either business or personal nature. It usually marks the start of a special event or occasion, such as a conference, a lecture, a workshop, or a celebration, where there needs to be a formal opening.

The purpose of a welcome speech is to make your guests feel part of the occasion and look forward to whatever is coming next, so it should be informative, complementary, and positive. It is also important to consider the audience and the nature of the event. Think about the common interests everybody shares and try to bring all your guests together by relating to these common interests. Although it is advisable to use a tone that is a pleasant mix of formal and informal, the general tone of the welcome speech should be in line with the mood and spirit of the event.

The following are some useful tips for planning a welcome speech:

- Open your speech by thanking everybody for coming to the event.
- Acknowledge specifically your important guests. If there are any special guests at the event, they should be welcomed and thanked for gracing the occasion with their presence.
- Mention, if appropriate, the goal of the event and the activities planned for the event. This will help to make your audience feel enthusiastic about the event at hand.
- Make a link between the event and the accomplishments of the special guests. Refer to the achievements of the individuals or group you are welcoming and thank them for their contribution to the event.
- Offer friendship and hospitality by saying some warm words. Say you hope they feel at home and enjoy the event.
- Thank all those people who have made the event possible before you end the speech.
- End your speech by wishing all, and especially the guests of honor, an interesting morning, afternoon or evening.

Before you give your speech, make sure you have got the names of all the special guests you need to welcome and make sure you know how to introduce them properly. Check all the facts you are going to mention about each of them and make sure they are factually correct.

It is appropriate to keep your welcome speech brief. A 1-to-3-minute speech is generally sufficient. Use the S-S-S formula for success: short, simple and sincere. Your listeners will appreciate it.

Questions to Think About

1. Why is it appropriate to mention the purpose of the event in a speech of welcome?

2. What is similar between a speech of introduction and a speech of welcome? What is different?

3. Suppose you are welcoming 1) an IT engineer, 2) an IT professor, 3) an IT company manager to a conference, what achievements of these individuals can you mention in your speech to make them feel valued and welcome?

Communication Tasks

1. Revise the speech of introduction you composed in the previous unit and change it into a speech of welcome.

2. Deliver your welcome speech in class and observe how your classmates respond to it. Then discuss with your classmate about how you can sound sincere when welcoming someone. Report the result of your discussion to your class.

3. On a more personal occasion such as a birthday party or a wedding anniversary, you might also need to make a welcome speech to greet the friends and guests. Search the Internet or your library to find a sample of welcome speech of a more personal nature. Practice the delivery of this sample speech.

Section C Exam Spotlight

Activity One

*Direction: In this section, you will hear three news reports **ONLY ONCE**. At the end of each news report, you will be given 10 seconds to answer the questions.*

News Item One

1. **A.** Having settled the country's finance problem.

B. Having increased the country's revenues.

C. Having paid more tax.

D. Having taken the place of other industries.

2. **A.** Discouraging investment at home.   **B.** Increasing oil prices.

   C. Attracting more foreign investment.   **D.** Changing the country's finance situation.

News Item Two

3. **A.** Houses.   **B.** Land.

   C. Skies.   **D.** Cars.

4. **A.** The fires were thought to have been started purposefully.

   B. The fires were thought to have been started accidentally.

   C. The fires were thought to have been started on the Mexican border.

   D. The fires were thought to have been started in southern California.

News Item Three

5. **A.** $14 billion.   **B.** $40 billion.

   C. $2.5 billion.   **D.** $25 billion.

6. **A.** The agricultural problem would influence the food security according to the FAO.

   B. The funds for meeting the climate change and food security problem are adequate.

   C. In many cases, the slowdown of agriculture could be recovered.

   D. It will take a long time and a large sum of money to reach the goal.

② Activity Two

Direction: In this section, you will hear part of a conversation in an English class. After listening, you are required to fill in the blanks with the exact words you have just heard.

M=Man   G=Girl

M: Today we will **7.** _____ concerning a very important word—heart. We will try to **8.** _____ to better understand the most important things about words. So take heart. **9.** _____ .

Besides, learning new words can be fun. There is no need for a heavy heart. Such feelings of sadness would only **10.** _____, or make me feel unhappy and hopeless. Now, let us suppose you and I were speaking freely about something private. Who can give me a sentence including "heart"? Mm... OK, Luna.

G: I might **11.** _____, or say things honestly and truthfully. I might even open up my heart to you and tell you a secret. I would speak with all my heart, or with great feeling. We would be having a heart-to-heart discussion.

M: Excellent! If we had an honest discussion, both of us would know that the other person's **12.** _____. For example, I would know that you are a kind-hearted and well-meaning person. And, if you are a very good person, I would even say that you have a heart of gold. However, you might **13.** _____ based on what I tell you. Our discussion might cause you to change the way you feel about something.

G: When a person shares her feelings freely and openly like this, you might say **14.** _____ _____, or on her clothing. Her emotions are not protected.

M: Exactly! But, let us suppose someone gets angry over what I say. Or worse, **15.** _____ _____ or understanding for me or my situation. If this happens, I might think that he **16.** _____. And, if you say something to make me frightened or worried, my heart might stand still or skip a beat.

G: My heart goes out to anyone who loses a friend over an argument. It really is a sad situation, and I feel sympathy for the people involved.

③ Activity Three

Direction: In this section, you will hear two long conversations. At the end of each conversation, you will be given 15 seconds to answer the questions.

Conversation One

17. **A.** To make an appointment.   **B.** To ask for an interview.

   C. To promote advertisement.   **D.** To have a negotiation.

18. **A.** Impatient but then reluctant.   **B.** Indifferent but then interested.

   C. Reluctant but then convinced.   **D.** Impatient but then accepted.

19. **A.** Customers can get the payment back if they're not satisfied with the products.

   B. The company will redo the products again and again until the costumers are satisfied.

C. Customers should do exactly according to the contract.

D. The company charges a proper amount of money.

Conversation Two

20. A. She has a temperature.　　　　　　**B.** She suffers from a headache.

　　C. She has a sore throat.　　　　　　　**D.** She often feels dizzy.

21. A. She didn't have enough sleep.　　　　**B.** She has caught a bad cold.

　　C. She is dying from a serious disease.　　**D.** She is too nervous to feel at home.

22. A. She should take some medicine and more water.

　　B. She should take care of her rest and drink more water.

　　C. She should give up her term paper for her health.

　　D. She should receive more check-up.

④ Activity Four

*Direction: In this section, you will hear a passage **THREE TIMES**. When the passage is read for the first time, you should listen carefully for its general idea. When the passage is read for the second time, you are required to fill in the blanks with the exact words you have just heard. Finally, when the passage is read for the third time, you should check what you have written.*

When most people think of the word "education", they think of a pupil as a sort of animate sausage casing. Into this empty casting, the teachers **23.** _____ stuff "education".

But genuine education, as Socrates knew more than two thousand years ago, is not **24.** _____ the stuffing of information into a person, but rather eliciting knowledge from him; it is the **25.** _____ of what is in the mind.

"The most important part of education," once wrote William Ernest Hocking, the **26.** _____ Harvard philosopher, "is the instruction of a man in what he has inside of him."

And, as Edith Hamilton has reminded us, Socrates never said, "I know, learn from me." He said, rather, "Look into your own selves and find the **27.** _____ of the truth that God has put into every heart and that only you can kindle to a **28.** _____."

In a dialogue, Socrates takes an ignorant slave boy, without a day of **29.** _____, and proves to the amazed observers that the boy really "knows" geometry—because the principles of

geometry are already in his mind, waiting to be called out.

So many of the discussions and **30.** _____ about the content of education are useless and inconclusive because they **31.** _____ what should "go into" the student rather than with what should be taken out, and how this can best be done.

The college student who once said to me, after a lecture, "I spend so much time studying that I don't have a chance to learn anything," was clearly expressing his **32.** _____ with the sausage casing view of education.

Unit 4
Gender Disparity in IT

Learning Objectives

- To learn further knowledge of occupation in IT
- To learn to find out the key ideas of listening materials
- To learn skills of debating

Section A Listening

Pre-Listening

Direction: Work in pairs and discuss the following questions.

1. What are the benefits of gender diversity in IT?

2. How does education affect female's participation in IT?

Warm-up Activities

⚙ Vocabulary

Edinburgh	['ɛdnˌbərə]	*n.*	the capital of Scotland; located in the Lothian Region on the south side of the Firth of Forth 爱丁堡（英国城市名）
quota	['kwotə]	*n.*	a prescribed number or a proportional share assigned to each participant 定额；配额
neutral	['nʊtrəl]	*adj.*	not supporting anyone in a disagreement, war, or contest, etc. 中立的；中性的
flourishing	['flɜrɪʃɪŋ]	*adj.*	growing or developing successfully 繁茂的；繁荣的

① Activity One

Direction: In this section, you will hear a news report. After listening, you should choose the best answer to each question. Now listen to the news report.

1. What is the news report mainly about?

    A. Gender disparity in IT occupations.

    B. The cause of gender disparity.

    C. Gender equality in computer applications.

    D. Gender equality has gained more importance.

2. Which place is **NOT** mentioned about the survey?

   A. Canada.   **B.** Vancouver.

   C. Alabama.   **D.** British.

3. According to the survey, what do women tend to believe?

   A. Lacking correlation between ability and career choice makes women unsuccessful in IT.

   B. Lacking necessary skills makes women unsuccessful in IT.

   C. Positive correlation between ability and career choice makes women successful in IT.

   D. Positive correlation between ability and career choice makes women important in IT.

➁ Activity Two

Direction: Listen to another news report and choose the best answer to each question.

4. What is the major point of the findings?

   A. Recruiting and intention techniques for women.

   B. Recruiting and retention techniques for those females having studied in the field.

   C. Research conducted in 48 separate case studies all over Europe.

   D. Research has 48 individual case studies across Europe.

5. Which is **NOT** mentioned about the range of these techniques?

   A. Advertisement campaigns.

   B. The allocation of quotas.

   C. The introduction of role models.

   D. Increasing the education body and technological facilities.

6. What does the previous generation think?

   A. IT would be a flourishing sector with multiple job opportunities.

   B. IT would be a flourishing sector with limited job opportunities.

   C. IT has many job opportunities for women.

   D. IT has limited job opportunities for men.

While-Listening

Text A — Statistics of Gender Disparity in Education and Workforce

⚙ Vocabulary

workforce	['wɜːkfɔːs]	*n.*	the group of people who work in a company, industry, country, etc. 劳动力
post-secondary	[ˌpost'sekəndεrɪ]	*adj.*	a level higher than middle school 中学以上的
SAT (Scholastic Aptitude Test)			an examination that American high school students take before they go to college 美国学术能力评估测验
spreadsheet	['spredʃit]	*n.*	a computer program, used especially in business, that allows you to do financial calculations and plans 电子数据表
literacy	['lɪtərəsɪ]	*n.*	the ability to read and write 读写能力
NSF (National Science Foundation)			美国国家科学基金会
Computing Research Association			计算机研究协会
Taulbee Survey			托比调查

① Activity One

Direction: In this section, you will hear a long passage. After listening, you should choose the best answer to each question. Now listen to the passage.

1. What happened in the mid-1980s?

   A. The proportion of women in computer science education decreased.

   B. The proportion of women in IT workforce soared up.

   C. The men in computer science education peaked.

   D. The men in IT workforce decreased.

2. What is the major point of NCWIT's report?

   A. Many SAT takers would rather not major in computer and information sciences.

    B. The proportion of girls intending to study computer and information sciences is less than that of boys.

    C. The proportion of girls intending to study computer and information sciences is larger than that of boys.

    D. Less of SAT takers would like to major in computer and information sciences.

3. According to a College Board report, which part is **NOT** mentioned about course work or experience?

    A. Computer literacy.   **B.** Internet activity.

    C. Word processing.   **D.** Creating websites.

4. How many boys and girls took the AP Computer Science A exam according to the College Board in 2006?

    A. 2,597 girls and 12,068 boys.   **B.** 2,594 girls and 12,680 boys.

    C. 2,945 girls and 12,860 boys.   **D.** 2,594 girls and 12,068 boys.

5. According to the report from NSF, what happened to female proportion?

    A. The percentage of women in IT areas declined from 33.1% to 29.6%.

    B. The percentage of women working as computer/information scientists increased from 29% to 33%.

    C. The percentage of men who held a bachelor's degree increased slightly.

    D. The percentage of men who had rich experience in S&E field declined slightly.

❷ Activity Two

Direction: Listen again and decide whether the following statements are true (T) or false (F).

6. In 1984, 37.1% of Computer Science degrees were awarded to females and the percentage dropped to 28.9% in 1989–1990, and 26.7% in 1997–1998. (　　)

7. Even now teenage girls are using computers at rates similar to their male peers, they are five times less likely to consider a technology-oriented career. (　　)

8. Of the 146,427 students who reported having no course work or experience, 61% were boys and 39% were girls. (　　)

9. From 1996 to 2004, females made up 16%–17% of those taking the AP Computer Science A exam and around 10% of those taking AP Computer Science AB exam. (　　)

10. A National Public Radio report in 2013 indicated that nearly 20% of all U.S. computer programmers are male. (　　)

Text B Bring Women into Computing

⚙ Vocabulary

underrepresentation	[ˈʌndəˌrɛprɪzɛnˈteʃən]	*n.*	the number of representatives is less than expectation 代表名额不足
initialize	[ɪˈnɪʃəlaɪz]	*vt.*	set the numbers, amounts, etc. in a computer program so that it is ready to start working 初始化
exposure	[ɪkˈspoʒɚ]	*n.*	the fact of experiencing something or being affected by it because of being in a particular situation or place 暴露；曝光
Carnegie Mellon University			卡耐基梅隆大学
British Computer Society (BCS)			英国计算机学会
Ontario	[ɑnˈtɛrɪo]		安大略湖（北美五大湖之一）
mentor	[ˈmɛntɔr]	*vt.*	serve as a trusted counselor or teacher to (another person) 指导

❶ Activity One

*Direction: In this section, you will hear a passage **ONLY ONCE**. While listening, you may write **NO MORE THAN THREE WORDS** for each gap. Make sure the word(s) you fill in is (are) both grammatically and semantically acceptable. Now listen to the passage.*

Bring Women into Computing

　　The **1.** _____ of data collected about women in IT has been **2.** _____, such as interviews and case studies. Many suggestions for incorporating more females into IT areas include formal mentoring, **3.** _____ opportunities, employee referral bonuses and other parts.

　　A research study was initialized by Allan Fisher and Jane Margolis, a social scientist and expert in **4.** _____ in education. The main issues discovered in women in computer science were feelings of experience gap, interest in curriculum and **5.** _____, and peer culture.

6. _____ exposures to early computer experiences, such as The Alice Project, are thought to be effective in terms of retention and creation of enthusiasm for women who may later consider entering the field. Besides, institutions of higher education are making changes regarding the process and **7.** _____ of mentoring to women that are undergraduates in technical fields.

Programs like all-girl computer camps and other activities for girls have been **8.** _____ _____ more interest at a younger age. A specific example of this kind of program is the Canadian Information Processing Society outreach program, in which a **9.** _____ is sent to schools in Canada.

In the U.S., the Association for Women in Computing was founded in Washington, D.C. in 1978. Through programs on technical and **10.** _____ topics, it made women more employed.

② Activity Two

Direction: Listen again and decide whether the following statements are true (T) or false (F).

11. The number of female college entrants stating interest in majoring in computer science decreased in the 2000s to pre-1880's levels. (   )

12. Universities across North America would not like to change their computer science programs for women. (   )

13. There is another strategy aimed to make more girls become integrated in majoring in computer science, that is to take early outreach to elementary and high-school girls. (   )

14. In the U.S., the Association for Women in Computing targets to provide opportunities for the professional growth of women in related areas. (   )

Post-Listening

Direction: Work in pairs and discuss the following questions.

1. How many barriers are there that women face in IT and computing?

2. Please explain psychological differences in your own words between genders in IT.

Section B Speaking

An Introduction to British Parliamentary Debate

Debate, in its simplest form, is an exchange of reasoned arguments for and against a proposition. In educational debate, the end result is determined by evaluating the cogency of each side's arguments. Public debate should give priority to logic while maintaining awareness of emotional appeals.

The British Parliamentary (BP) debating is the format used by most university competitions at home and abroad. In a BP debate, the speakers are given only fifteen minutes' notice of the motion, which is the issue for discussion and debating. Speeches are usually between five and seven minutes in duration.

Teams in a BP Debate

The debate consists of four teams of two speakers, called *factions*, with two factions on either side of the case. Because of its origins in British parliamentary procedure, the two sides in a BP debate are called the *Government* and *Opposition*, while the speakers take their titles from those of their parliamentary equivalents, so the opening Government speaker is called the *Prime Minister*. The other speakers are similarly titled:

1. Opening Government (first faction):

    (1) Prime Minister

    (2) Deputy Prime Minister

2. Opening Opposition (second faction):

    (1) Leader of the Opposition

    (2) Deputy Leader of the Opposition

3. Closing Government (third faction):

    (1) Member for the Government

    (2) Government Whip

4. Closing Opposition (fourth faction):

    (1) Member for the Opposition

    (2) Opposition Whip

The Turn of Speaking in a BP Debate

Each team is allocated whether they will propose or oppose the motion. Speaking alternates between the two sides and the order of the debate is therefore:

1. Prime Minister

2. Opposition Leader

3. Deputy Prime Minister

4. Deputy Opposition Leader

5. Member for the Government

6. Member for the Opposition

7. Government Whip

8. Opposition Whip

Speaker Roles

Each speaker has a role and each speech has a specific purpose. All speakers, except the final speakers for the Proposition and Opposition (Proposition and Opposition Whips), should introduce new material. All debaters should refute the opposing teams' arguments, except the Prime Minister.

The Prime Minister should: 1) define the motion; 2) outline the case he and his partner will put forward and explain which speaker will deal with which arguments; 3) develop his own arguments, which should be separated into two or three main points; 4) finish by summarizing his main points.

The Leader of Opposition should: 1) respond to the definition if it is unfair or makes no link to the motion; 2) rebut the first proposition speech; 3) outline the case which the Opposition will put forward and explain which speakers will deal with which arguments; and 4) offer additional arguments (roughly two) about why the policy is a bad idea, or develop a counter case.

The Deputy Prime Minister should rebut the response made by the Leader of Opposition and rebut his/her main arguments. Moreover, the Deputy Prime Minister should develop his own arguments separated into two or three main points and conclude with a summary of the whole team case.

The Deputy Leader of Opposition, in turn, should rebut the speech of the second proposition speaker, and offer some more arguments to support the Opposition's approach to the motion. The Deputy Leader of Opposition also need to summarize the case for the team.

The Member of the Government should, apart from rebuttal, extend the debate into a new area and introduce a couple of new arguments that make the case more persuasive. This is quite a complex part of the BP debating, but it is very important to add something new to the debate or you will be penalized.

Likewise, the Member of the Opposition must, apart from rebuttal, also bring an extension to the debate, in other words, to extend the debate into a new area or bring in a couple of new arguments to rebut the new analysis of the third proposition speaker.

The Government Whip makes the last speech (on the side of the Government) known as a summary speech. The speaker should step back and look at the debate as a whole and explain why on all the areas you have made good arguments to win over the Opposition side. The whip speech may go through the debate chronologically, or side by side, or point by point, explaining why each of the main issues have been won by your side.

The Opposition Whip's duty is very much like that of the closing proposition. The last opposition speaker must devote the whole speech to a summing up and should not introduce new material.

Points of Information

Points of Information (POI) are interjections made by members directed at the speech of the member holding the floor, and made from a sitting position. The BP debate demands that all speakers offer POIs to their opposition. POIs are important as it allows the first two factions to maintain their relevance during the course of the debate, and the last two factions to introduce their arguments early in the debate. The first and last minute of each speech is considered "protected time", during which no points of information may be offered.

Case Building

Many teams find it difficult to come up with a good case statement and supporting arguments. You should identify your contention/case statement (even if it's just a rewording of the resolution) in a one sentence. For example, if the motion is: This House would legalize euthanasia, your case statement can be: The proposition will argue that doctors in the U.K. should be allowed to administer lethal drugs to terminally ill patients. Having identified the case statement, all you need to do is answer the following two questions: 1) Why should we implement this resolution? and, 2) How would we implement this resolution? Then your case will be effectively built. You may also use the problem-cause-solution order and the Monroe's Motivated Sequence to build your case on a policy debate.

Ⓛ Questions to Think About

1. Why do you think in a BP debate, debaters should take turns to speak? What is the advantage of this kind of format?

2. Which speaking role do you consider to be the most challenging? Why?

3. What do you think is the task of the Government Whip and the Opposition Whip respectively during the debate?

4. In building your case, you need to have an effective case statement. Is the case statement different from the position statement in a persuasive speech?

Communication Tasks

1. Work in pairs. Try to build your case on the side of both the Government and the Opposition, using the following motions:

   (1) This House believes that the shortage of women professionals in IT is a result of women's choice.

   (2) This House believes that the gender imbalance in IT will affect innovation.

   (3) This House believes that success can be copied despite gender differences.

2. Use one of the following motions to stage a BP debate in groups. You may have a few days to prepare for it.

   (1) This House would set a quota for women workers in IT companies.

   (2) This House believes that the creation of feminist icons in IT is good for gender equality in IT.

   (3) This House believes that taxi e-hailing apps should be banned.

   (4) This House would make fathers take paternity leave.

   (5) This House believes that the international community should cut off Internet access in Syria.

Section C Exam Spotlight

Activity One

*Direction: In this section, you will hear two telephone conversations **TWICE**. After listening, write one or two words in each blank.*

Conversation One

Personplan Employment Agency

Message

Date and time of message: 18/5/2004   9:30 a.m.

Caller: Mary Jones

Name of Company: Jack Strong Inc.

Staff required: **1.** _____

Skills required: **2.** _____   **3.** _____

To start work: **4.** _____

Contact number: (212) 562 6030

Conversation Two

Catering Services Department

Message

To: Elizabeth   Date: 5/12/2004

Time: 2:30 p.m.

Mr. Moss from **5.** _____ Division rang. He wants to order a dinner on

6. _____ for 15. He wants it served in the **7.** _____ dinning room

with at least three **8.** _____. Can you get back to him as soon as possible?

② Activity Two

*Direction: In this section, you will hear a passage **THREE TIMES**. When the passage is read for the first time, you should listen carefully for its general idea. When the passage is read for the second time, you are required to fill in the blanks with either the exact words you have just heard or the main points in your own words. Finally, when the passage is read for the third time, you should check what you have written.*

The Internet makes our world a small **9.** _____. It also makes me understand that the generation gap **10.** _____ not only between the young and the old, but also among the young, even though there are only three or five year gaps in age.

I was born in the 70's, and I always had new ideas and passions when I was in college. Now, I brought my passion to my work and I **11.** _____ that I had kept my youth and that there was not a gap between the **12.** _____ generation of the 80's and mine.

Last Friday, I invited one friend to **13.** _____ my home. He felt **14.** _____ when I **15.** _____ him that many students make friends on the Internet. In his memory, **16.** _____.

Actually, present students can find a partner for sports, for study, for discussion, or for traveling online. They can even find a boyfriend or girlfriend on the net.

17. _____.

They are crazier than we were. They have more passion for life. **18.** _____

_____.

③ Activity Three

Direction: In this section, you will hear two long conversations. At the end of each conversation, you will be given 15 seconds to answer the questions.

Conversation One

19. **A.** They lived in caves.
    C. They had an advanced language.
    B. They traveled in groups.
    D. They ate mostly fruit.

20. **A.** They lived in large groups.
    C. They kept fires burning constantly.
    B. They used sand as insulation.
    D. They faced their homes toward the south.

21. **A.** Meet his anthropology teacher.
    B. Lend him her magazine when she's done with it.
    C. Come over to his house after class.
    D. Help him study for an anthropology test.

Conversation Two

22. **A.** Register when they arrive.
    C. Register their guests.
    B. Bring up to three guests.
    D. Show membership cards on arrival.

23. **A.** There is no charge for using the lockers.
    B. Twenty cents should be paid for using the lockers.
    C. Clothes are not advised to leave in the lockers.
    D. It is safer to bring the clothes than leave them in the lockers.

24. A. For 30 minutes only.   **B.** For one hour only.

C. Within the booked time only.   **D.** Longer than the booked time.

④ Activity Four

Direction: *In this section, you will hear a conversation **ONLY ONCE**. After listening, you should fill in the blanks. Now listen to the conversation.*

—Sandra wanted the tutor to get some **25.** _____ on her group's trip guideline. Then, she need to be careful of avoiding typos and problems with layout **26.** _____.

—The tutor has made several notes on the proposal. It could have been **27.** _____.

—The tutor has **28.** _____ the proposal and she thinks Sandra has used complex structure and other things for the sake of it and **29.** _____.

—The tutor reminds Sandra of remembering to include **30.** _____, which are important and make ideas clearly.

—Sandra wanted to go to the destination to see **31.** _____, many of which were shot there. Because it is awesome **32.** _____.

—Sandra wondered whether her proposal was **33.** _____.

—Sandra described that the way they **34.** _____ from the flat landscape is just amazing.

Unit 5
Network Security

Learning Objectives

- To learn to use proper words to talk about Internet security
- To learn to listen for detailed information in listening materials
- To learn to demonstrate a process

Section Ⓐ Listening

Pre-Listening

Direction: Work in pairs and discuss the following questions.

1. Do you have the awareness of Internet security protection?

2. Have you heard of cyber attack? What do you know about it?

Warm-up Activities

⚙ Vocabulary

tow truck   ['to'trʌk]   *n.*   a truck equipped to hoist and pull wrecked cars (or to remove cars from no-parking zones) 拖车

① Activity One

Direction: In this section, you will hear the first part of a passage. After listening, you should choose the best answer to each question. Now listen to the passage.

1. Which month is the Cyber Security Awareness Month?

   A. May.   **B.** June.   **C.** October.   **D.** December.

2. How many pages are there in the guide?

   A. 10 pages.   **B.** 20 pages.   **C.** 30 pages.   **D.** 40 pages.

3. How many news jobs does the small businesses create in 2009?

   A. About 40 percent of the country's new jobs.

   B. About 45 percent of the country's new jobs.

   C. About 50 percent of the country's new jobs.

   D. About 95 percent of the country's new jobs.

➋ Activity Two

Direction: Listen to the rest of the passage and decide whether the following statements are true (T)
or false (F).

4. Unlike big companies, the computers at small businesses hold sensitive information on customers, employees and business partners. (   )

5. The guide provides 10 "absolutely necessary steps" to secure information. (   )

6. There are no appendices in the guide. (   )

While-Listening

Text A People Disregard Security Warnings on Computers

⚙ Vocabulary

pop up	['pɑp'ʌp]	*v.*	appear suddenly or unexpectedly 突然出现
disregard	[ˌdɪsrɪ'gɑrd]	*vt.*	give little or no attention to 无视；不顾
whopping	['wɑpɪŋ]	*adj.*	(used informally) very large 巨大的，庞大的
haphazardly	[hæp'hæzədlɪ]	*adv.*	in a random manner 随意地；杂乱无章地
status quo	[ˌstetəs'kwo]	*n.*	the existing state of affairs 现状
random	['rændəm]	*adj.*	lacking any definite plan or order or purpose; governed by or depending on chance 随意的
neural	['nʊrəl]	*adj.*	of or relating to the nervous system 神经的

➊ Activity One

*Direction: In this section, you will hear a passage **ONLY ONCE**. While listening, you may write **NO***
*   ***MORE THAN THREE WORDS** for each gap. Make sure the word(s) you fill in is (are)*
*   *both grammatically and semantically acceptable. Now listen to the passage.*

A. Researchers found these times are less **1.** _____ because of "dual task **2.** _____",
a neural **3.** _____ where even simple tasks can't be simultaneously performed without
4. _____ performance loss.

B. We found that the brain can't handle **5.** _____ very well.

C. And a whopping 87 percent disregarded the messages while they were **6.** _____ information, in this case, a **7.** _____ code.

D. Waiting to **8.** _____ a warning to when people are not busy doing something else increases their security behavior **9.** _____ .

② Activity Two

Direction: Listen again and decide whether the following statements are true (T) or false (F).

10. A new study finds that the status quo of warning messages appearing haphazardly results in up to 90 percent of users disregarding them. ( )

11. 74 percent of people in the study ignored security messages if they were watching a video. ( )

12. People pay the most attention to security messages when they pop up in higher dual task times. ( )

13. Timing security warnings to appear when a person is more likely ready to respond isn't current practice in the software industry. ( )

14. The experiment showed neural activity was slightly reduced when security messages interrupted a task, as compared to when a user responded to the security message itself. ( )

Text B — Security Flaw Could Reach Beyond Websites to Digital Devices

⚙ Vocabulary

flaw	[flɔ]	*n.*	an imperfection in a device or machine 瑕疵；缺点
gut	[gʌt]	*n.*	essential (mechanical) part of something 某物的重要（机械）部分
server	['sɜ·və·]	*n.*	(computer science) a computer that provides client stations with access to files and printers as shared resources to a computer network 服务器

configure	[kən'fɪgjə·]	*v.*	set up for a particular purpose 配置
fallout	['fɔlaʊt]	*n.*	any adverse and unwanted secondary effect 后果；余波
router	['rʊtə·]	*n.*	(computer science) a device that forwards data packets between computer networks 路由器
nasty	['næstɪ]	*adj.*	dangerous; threatening 危险的；威胁的

➊ Activity One

Direction: In this section, you will hear a passage. After listening, you should decide whether the following statements are true (T) or false (F). Now listen to the passage.

1. Security experts said the potential of Heartbleed bug for harm could extend much further, to the guts of the Internet and the many devices that connect to it. (   )

2. Juniper Networks said its products were not affected. (   )

3. Chuck Mulloy, a spokesman for Intel, said they had found no vulnerabilities so far. (   )

4. OpenSSL is built into some of the hardware like home routers and printers. (   )

5. Security researchers say that there have been an increase in black market sales of sensitive data, like passwords. (   )

➋ Activity Two

Direction: Listen again and choose the best answer to each question.

6. Which kind of products Cisco makes were **NOT** affected?

   A. Some kinds of phones that connect to the Internet.

   B. A kind of server that helps people conduct online meetings.

   C. A kind of device used for office communications.

   D. Its online servers.

7. What does OpenSSL do?

   A. It helps save information on the Internet.

   B. It helps protect information on the Internet.

C. It helps encrypt information on the Internet.

D. It helps steal information on the Internet.

8. All of the following are the reasons why OpenSSL being built into some hardware is a nasty problem, except _____.

   A. OpenSSL is built into some of this hardware like home routers and printers connected to the Internet.

   B. The web—with sites like Facebook and Google—is the most visible part of the Internet.

   C. OpenSSL goes far beyond just websites.

   D. OpenSSL is implemented in email protocols and all kinds of embedded devices.

9. Why was most of the equipment made by Cisco and Juniper unaffected?

   A. Because they did not use OpenSSL for their encryption.

   B. Because the companies don't make home routers.

   C. Because they have protection systems.

   D. Because they are immune from the bug.

10. According to Mr. Kurtz, if users want to be absolutely secure, what are they advised to do?

    A. Stop using OpenSSL.

    B. Change a new home router.

    C. Check with their home router manufacturers to upgrade their devices.

    D. Upgrade their software.

Post-Listening

Direction: Work in pairs and discuss the following questions.

1. Will you ignore the security messages when they pop up on web pages?

2. Have you ever been hacked? Can you give some ideas on how to avoid being hacked?

Section **B** Speaking

Demonstrating a Process

To show is worth a thousand words. An effective demonstration is the best way of teaching someone how to do something step by step. Speeches that demonstrate how to do something by steps are very similar to a user's manual or instructions, but the speaker actually carries out the steps and finishes the process while speaking about it. The purpose of this type of speech is to clarify the steps in the procedure so that the audience can recreate the steps and the results. A good demonstration allows the audience to try out what is being demonstrated, if not during the speech itself, then later on their own.

However, topics for speeches that demonstrate need to be chosen with care. A difficult task cannot be adequately and clearly demonstrated in a few minutes. Few of us can learn to operate a microscope, for example, by simply watching a speaker demonstrate the activity just once. On the other hand, the operation of a microwave oven can be the subject of demonstration, for it can be learned in a reasonably short time by following simple steps.

The first thing to do to make your demonstration effective is careful preparation. You need to get all the materials ready and prepared. It would also be helpful if you can provide some handouts (like a written recipe) and some form of visual aid (like a PowerPoint or some photos) to help your audience learn and remember the steps.

Since a process speech describes a sequence of steps, it is important that the steps be demonstrated in the order that they occur; in other words, the steps should be arranged in chronological order. In a process speech, ordering steps chronologically is vital, especially if the audience is to recreate the process.

Generally speaking, most processes break down into a beginning (introduction), middle (development), and end (conclusion). The introductory part should introduce the topic and establish the purpose for the speech. The actual demonstration of the process, which is usually made up of three to five major steps, is the middle part of the speech. Don't include too many steps in one demonstration, for you may confuse your audience. Finally, to conclude the speech, you can show the results of the process and encourage your audience to try the steps out on their own.

In addition, while demonstrating the process, make sure the demonstration is visible to the audience. Your audience need to see clearly what you do with your hands or which key or button to press.

Questions to Think About

1. Topics for speeches that demonstrate need to be chosen with care. Discuss with your classmates and decide on three possible topics for demonstration. Explain to your classmates why you believe a certain topic is good or bad.

2. Search the Internet and find the recipe of your favorite dish. How many steps are there in the cooking process? Sort them out.

3. Are you good at DIY activities? Are you good at doing anything that is easy to learn and worthy of learning? How would you demonstrate the process of doing it to your classmates and friends?

Communication Tasks

1. Use the recipe of your favorite dish and compose a speech demonstrating how to make the dish. Prepare all necessary materials and ingredients and demonstrate the cooking process to your classmates.

2. Work in a group of three or four and demonstrate the complex process of making a purchase online. Break this process down into three parts: 1) creating your account, 2) selecting the goods you want, and 3) making the payment online. Select one person to do each part with the help of a PPT.

3. Work in pairs. One student show the other how to do something he/she is good at so that the other learns how to do it. Then decide which student does a better job demonstrating and why.

Section C Exam Spotlight

Activity One

*Direction: In this section, you will hear two telephone conversations **TWICE**. After listening, write one or two words in each blank.*

Conversation One

Memo

To: Ms. **1.** _____

From: Williams Smith

Type of job applied for: **2.** _____

Time of interview: **3.** _____ tomorrow.

Location of the company: **4.** _____ Washington Street.

Conversation Two

Message

From: Bill's **5.** _____ Company

Re: arrange a **6.** _____

Time: 6:00 p.m. next **7.** _____ afternoon

Consumption standard: **8.** _____ per head

---

② Activity Two

*Direction: In this section, you will hear a passage **THREE TIMES**. When the passage is read for the first time, you should listen carefully for its general idea. When the passage is read for the second time, you are required to fill in the blanks with the exact words you have just heard. Finally, when the passage is read for the third time, you should check what you have written.*

Many teachers all over the world play music to students in class. Many are inspired by the belief that hearing music can boost IQ in **9.** _____ tasks, the so-called Mozart effect. While the evidence actually suggests it's a stretch to say classical music boosts **10.** _____, researchers do think pleasant sounds before a task can sometimes **11.** _____ and help you perform well. The key appears to be that you enjoy what you're hearing. "If you like the music or you like the sound, even listening to a Stephen King novel, then you did better. It didn't matter about the music," researchers say.

However, it's worth considering that music is not always helpful while you're trying to work. Trying to perform a task which **12.** _____ serial recall, for instance, doing **13.** _____ arithmetic, will be impaired by sounds with acoustic variation, which includes most types of music. Songs with **14.** _____, on the other hand, are more likely to **15.** _____ tasks that involve semantics—such as reading **16.** _____.

"The task and the sound are important, when you have both of them using the same process, then you get problems," researchers say. So, it seems that schools that choose to create **17.** _____ soundscapes could enhance the learning of their students, **18.** _____ they make careful choices.

③ Activity Three

Direction: In this section, you will hear two long conversations. At the end of each conversation, you will be given 15 seconds to answer the questions.

Conversation One

19. A. In a hotel.　　　　　　　　　　　　**B.** At a restaurant.

　　C. In a travel agency.　　　　　　　　　**D.** In a shop.

20. A. With a credit card.　　　　　　　　　**B.** With traveler's cheques.

　　C. With cash in the local currency.　　　　**D.** With cash in U.S. dollars.

21. A. The waitress gives it to the customer in American dollars.

　　B. The waitress gives it to the customer in the local currency.

　　C. The customer leaves the change for the waitress as there isn't much left.

　　D. There is no change because the customer doesn't pay the bill in cash.

Conversation Two

22. A. Giving a lecture.　　　　　　　　　　**B.** Discussing political science.

　　C. Working on a science problem.　　　　**D.** Reading twentieth-century literature.

23. A. They make him feel good.　　　　　　**B.** They make no impact on him.

　　C. They bore him.　　　　　　　　　　　**D.** They make him angry.

24. A. Professor Hawl is a controversial figure on campus.

　　B. Professor Hawl plays an important part in college.

　　C. Students admire Professor Hawl for his wonderful lectures.

　　D. Students are sleepy in Professor Hawl's lecture.

④ Activity Four

*Direction: In this section, you will hear a passage **ONLY ONCE**. While listening, you may write **NO MORE THAN THREE WORDS** for each gap. Make sure the word(s) you fill in is (are) both grammatically and semantically acceptable. Now listen to the passage.*

Built to Fail?

Do manufacturers design technology so that it eventually fails? Or is it just that consumers expect less these days? Professor Cooper, an expert in sustainable consumption and production at Nottingham Trent University, tries to explore people's relationship with buying new technology.

Suffering from a "throwaway culture", a culture in which people **25.** _____ much more easily, and which is not good for **26.** _____, he first took mobile phones as one example. He says that mobile phones' screens **27.** _____ often and generally when that happens people buy a new one. That's partly because mobile phones' screens are **28.** _____ on rather than screwed on, which is designed by the manufacturers deliberately. He thinks that generally, people have **29.** _____ when it comes to how long things should last. By way of an example, Professor Cooper says that his parents' washing machine lasted for 37 years. These days, they last between five and ten. People don't see electrical products as an **30.** _____ in the same way that people used to. People now worry that what they buy today will become **31.** _____ tomorrow.

Cooper suggests that if people can afford it, people really should try to buy higher quality products. And manufacturers should **32.** _____ on their products saying how long they are designed to last.

Unit 6
Cyber Attack and Cyber Bullying

Learning Objectives

- To learn information about cyber attack
- To learn to grasp key words
- To learn to deal with long passages
- To learn some skills of making a persuasive speech

Section Ⓐ Listening

Pre-Listening

Direction: Work in pairs and discuss the following questions.

1. What is cyber attack?
2. Can you give some examples about the advantages and disadvantages of Internet?

Warm-up Activities

⚙ Vocabulary

typewriter	['taɪpraɪtə˞]	*n.*	A typewriter is a machine with keys which are pressed in order to print letters, numbers, or other characters onto paper. 打字机
register	['rɛdʒɪstə˞]	*vt.*	If you register to do something, you put your name on an official list, in order to be able to do that thing or to receive a service. 登记；注册；记录
laser	['lezə˞]	*n.*	A laser is a narrow beam of concentrated light produced by a special machine. It is used for cutting very hard materials, and in many technical fields such as surgery and telecommunications. 激光
virus	['vaɪərəs]	*n.*	A virus is a kind of germ that can cause disease. 病毒
webcam	['wɛb'kæm]	*n.*	A webcam is a video camera that takes pictures which can be viewed on a website. The pictures are often of something that is happening while you watch. 网络摄像头
statistically	[stə'tɪstɪklɪ]	*adv.*	Statistically means relating to the use of statistics. 统计地；统计学上

❶ Activity One

Direction: In this section, you will hear a passage. After listening, you should choose the best answer to each question. Now listen to the passage.

1. Why did you have to register if you owned a typewriter in the 1980s in the communist Eastern Germany?

    A. Because people could find it when it was stolen.

    B. Because the government could track the texts created by the typewriter.

    C. Because registering made the page unique.

    D. Because we couldn't understand it.

2. According to the passage, what is the influence of registering of typewriter?

    A. Creating wrong thoughts.

    B. Making the people in their countries different with people of communist Eastern Germany.

    C. Restricting freedom of speech.

    D. Letting people make fuss of it.

3. Which of the following is one of the main sources of online problems today?

    A. Light yellow dots printed on every single page.

    B. The governments are using technology against the citizens.

    C. People don't care about the print technology.

    D. People can't buy a different printer.

❷ Activity Two

Direction: Listen to another passage and choose the best answer to each question.

4. What is the basic suggestion given by the speaker?

    A. Not to download any viruses shown by the speaker.

    B. To know what a cyber security specialist looks like.

    C. Not to go to any website infected.

    D. To use the Internet in a right way.

5. According to the passage, what are the computer viruses unable to do?

    A. To steal the data.   **B.** To steal the money.

C. To monitor the user.   **D.** To stop the cybercrime.

6. Which kind of websites is most seriously infected by the computer virus?

    A. The porn sites.

    B. The small business websites.

    C. The websites related to power, utilities and infrastructure.

    D. The shopping websites.

While-Listening

Text A Everyday Cybercrime and What You Can Do About It

⚙ Vocabulary

spotty	['spɑtɪ]	*adj.*	Someone who is spotty has spots on their face. 发疹的；多斑点的
notoriety	[notə'raɪətɪ]	*n.*	To achieve notoriety means to become well known for something bad. 恶名；声名狼藉；丑名
tricky	['trɪkɪ]	*adj.*	If you describe a task or problem as tricky, you mean that it is difficult to do or deal with. 棘手的；难处理的
installation	[ɪnstə'leʃ(ə)n]	*n.*	the act of installing something 安装；装置
staggering	['stægərɪŋ]	*adj.*	Something that is staggering is very surprising. 惊人的，令人震惊的

❶ Activity One

Direction: In this section, you will hear a speech. After listening, you should choose the best answer to each question. Now listen to the speech.

1. Which of the following statements is **NOT** right about the cybercriminals?

    A. They are wonderfully professional and organized.

    B. They have the product adverts.

C. They work in the basement.

D. You can buy the services from them.

2. What can we get about the Black Hole Exploit Pack?

   A. It's the market leader in malware distribution.

   B. Half of the malware distribution is completed by it.

   C. It will attack your computer with video.

   D. It will attack its own website.

3. According to the speech, what do we need to think about when we adopt new applications and mobile devices?

   A. Whether they are good enough or not.

   B. The number of the people who are using them.

   C. How much we are spending on them.

   D. Personal privacy and security.

4. Why are the legal issues in the area of cybercriminals challenging?

   A. Because legal issues in this area are complicated.

   B. Because cybercriminals steal lots of money.

   C. Because cybercriminals can hide anywhere in the world.

   D. Because Internet is borderless while most laws are only implemented within a country.

5. What can we do to prevent malware from working?

   A. To see some astonishing stories in the news.

   B. To know that malware are doing incredible, terrifying and scary things.

   C. To do some basics, such as updating your computer and get a secure password.

   D. To ask the specialists for help.

❷ Activity Two

Direction: Listen again and decide whether the following statements are true (T) or false (F).

6. The cybercriminals could get lots of products and services, including a testing platform. (   )

7. More crimes packed with business intelligence reporting dashboards because cybercriminals want to manage the distribution of their malicious code. (   )

8. When you install something, look at the settings and make sure they are suitable for your computers or phones. (　　)

9. Despite of difficulties, the cybercriminals who steal millions of dollars have been arrested. (　　)

10. The majority of malware work because they are too strong. (　　)

Text B Three Types of Online Attack

⚙ Vocabulary

motive	['motɪv]	*n.*	Your motive for doing something is your reason for doing it. 动机，目的
plausible	['plɔzəbəl]	*adj.*	An explanation or statement that is plausible seems likely to be true or valid. 貌似可信的
certificate	[sə'tɪfɪkeɪt]	*n.*	A certificate is an official document stating that particular facts are true. 证书；执照；文凭
SSL (Security Socket Layer)			加密套接字协议层（一种加密的通讯协定，用在使用者与网服器之间）
encrypt	[ɪn'krɪpt]	*v.*	If a document or piece of information is encrypted, it is written in a special code, so that only certain people can read it. 将……译成密码
totalitarian	[toˌtælə'teriən]	*adj.*	of a system of government in which there is only one political party and no rival parties are allowed 极权主义的
dissident	['dɪsɪdənt]	*n.*	Dissidents are people who disagree with and criticize their government, especially because it is undemocratic. 持不同政见者；意见不同的人
trustworthy	['trʌs(t)wɜːðɪ]	*adj.*	reliable 可靠的；可信赖的
investigate	[ɪn'vestɪgeɪt]	*v.*	If someone, especially an official, investigates an event, situation, or claim, they try to find out what happened or what is the truth. 调查；研究

❶ Activity One

*Direction: In this section, you will hear a talk **ONLY ONCE**. While listening, you may write **NO MORE THAN THREE WORDS** for each gap. Make sure the word(s) you fill in is (are) both grammatically and semantically acceptable. Now listen to the talk.*

Three Types of Online Attack

Online attacks could be classified based on the **1.** _____.

We actually have several cases of **2.** _____. These guys make their fortunes online, but they make it through the **3.** _____ of using things like **4.** _____ to steal money from our bank accounts while we do online banking, or with key loggers to collect **5.** _____ while we are doing online shopping from an **6.** _____ . So it's more likely to become the victim of a **7.** _____ than here in the real world. In the future, the **8.** _____ will be happening online.

The second major group of attackers are not motivated by money. They're motivated by something else—motivated **9.** _____ , motivated **10.** _____ , motivated by the laughs.

❷ Activity Two

Direction: Listen again and decide whether the following statements are true (T) or false (F).

11. Anonymous is a group of attackers which is motivated by the money. (　　)

12. There are three main attackers: criminals for the money, hacktivists for the protest, and the Western government. (　　)

13. The dissidents in the countries like Iran like Gmail, because it is more reliable. (　　)

14. Only the totalitarian governments would use attack tools against their own citizens. (　　)

15. State Trojan could infect your computer and enables user to watch all your communication, to listen to your online discussions, and to collect your passwords. (　　)

16. A legal citizen doesn't need to care about the investigation from the government. (　　)

Post-Listening

Direction: Work in pairs and discuss the following questions.

1. In your opinion, which type of online attack is the worst?

2. How can we deal with the online attack?

Section B Speaking

Persuasive Speeches on a Public Policy

Have you ever made a speech to put forward a motion or a proposal concerning the management of your school or a family issue, or when you are running for chair of the student union? What was your motion? How did you put forward the blueprint of your policies?

A policy is a program or a sequence of actions adopted by social groups, governments, political parties or business organizations. Policy can influence, guide and determine decisions and actions. A speech on a public policy is about whether or not a specific course of action should be taken. For example, a speech to persuade the audience that special laws must be made and enforced in order to prevent and stop cyber bullying is a public policy speech.

In a public policy speech, the speaker can have two purposes: to win agreement of the audience and further, to elicit immediate action on the part of the audience. That is to say, the speaker must convince the audience the merits of his/her ideas and then move the audience to action in support of the policy.

The three basic issues to be covered in a speech of public policy include: the need for a policy, the policy itself and the feasibility of the policy.

There is no point in arguing for a policy unless you can show a need for it. So your first step is to identity a problem calling for a new policy as a solution. The second basic issue of policy speeches is to explain the policy or the plan you are proposing and show how it is going to effectively address the problem. This part deals with the issues of "what to do" and "how to do" to solve the existing problem. The third basic issue of policy speeches is feasibility or practicality of the policy. Once you have presented a plan, you must show that it will and can work without creating new and more serious problems.

In addition, effective organization is crucial when you seek to persuade listeners on a question of policy. Two organization schemes are especially useful for policy speeches: the problem-cause-solution order and the Monroe's Motivated Sequence.

Problem-cause-solution order: Your speech will be developed in three main parts. In the first main part, you demonstrate the problem and the need for a new policy. In the second main part, you analyze the causes of such problem. And then you explain your plan for solving the problem, showing your plan is practical and effective because it targets the causes. Following this order, a sample speech outline is given as follows:

Specific Purpose: *To persuade my audience that colleges and universities should take stronger action to control cyber bullying.*

Part I (problem): *Cyber bullying and victimization on college campus is a serious problem that needs to be addressed right away.*

Part II (cause): *There are three major causes specific to college life for the growth of cyber bullying targeting students.*

Part III (solution): *An effective solution must deal with all three major causes of the problem.*

The Monroe's Motivated Sequence: In this organization pattern, the speech is divided into five parts:

1. Attention: Gain the attention of the audience.

2. Need: Make the audience feel a need for change.

3. Satisfaction: Satisfy the sense of need by providing a solution to the problem.

4. Visualization: Intensify desire for the solution by visualizing its benefits.

5. Action: Urge the audience to take action in support of the solution.

The problem-cause-solution order and the Monroe's Motivated Sequence have proved to be clear and effective on countless policy issues. Try it out and you will find it can work for your speech, too.

Questions to Think About

1. What do you think is the connection between a value speech and a policy speech? Are they fundamentally different?

2. How would you decide how much of your speech should be devoted to need, policy and feasibility?

3. What are the similarities and differences between the problem-cause-solution order and the Monroe's Motivated Sequence?

4. Why is it essential to prove the feasibility of the policy you propose?

5. Which do you think would be more effective for a sales pitch, the problem-cause-solution order or the Monroe's Motivated Sequence? Why?

Communication Tasks

1. Conduct a survey to find out information about the problem of cyber bullying on university campus. Try to define the various causes of this problem, and then propose a policy to address this problem.

2. Using the information in the previous task and make a speech plan either following the problem-cause-solution order or the Monroe's Motivated Sequence.

3. Develop a speech outline either in the problem-cause-solution order or the Monroe's Motivated Sequence, using one of the topics below:

   (1) Teenage smoking

   (2) Online voting

   (3) Identity theft crimes online

   (4) Sexually-explicit media content

4. Choose the outline you think best and compose a speech of policy. Deliver the speech to your class.

Section C Exam Spotlight

Activity One

*Direction: In this section, you will hear three news reports **ONLY ONCE**. At the end of each news report, you will be given 10 seconds to answer the questions.*

News Item One

1. **A.** To cure the disease HIV/AIDS completely.

    B. To sentence people death penalties.

    C. To make HIV/AIDS treatable to some extent.

    D. To warn people to be cautious of HIV/AIDS.

2. **A.** They are first used by PEPFAR to treat HIV/AIDS.

    B. Their effectiveness makes PEPFAR benefit a lot.

    C. Their high cost would have influence on PEPFAR.

    D. They are copied from drugs of big drug companies.

News Item Two

3. **A.** Morgan Freeman.   **B.** Martin Scorsese.

    C. Clint Eastwood.   **D.** Hilary Swank.

4. **A.** Jamies Foxx.   **B.** Kate Blanchett.

    C. Hilary Swank.   **D.** Clint Eastwood.

News Item Three

5. **A.** The American president appeals to ban gun use in the U.S.

    B. The American president tries to stop gun violence in the U.S.

    C. Family members of gun victims meet to protest in the U.S.

    D. Parents are worried about their children's gun abuse in the U.S.

6. **A.** More than 500.   **B.** More than 30,000.

    C. More than 2,000.   **D.** Too many to count.

──

②Activity Two

Direction: In this section, you will hear a conversation. For questions 7 to 12, you should fill in the blanks. For questions 13 to 16, you should decide whether the statements are true (T), false (F) or not given (NG).

Mr. Smith comes to London for a **7.** _____. He will stay there for **8.** _____ of months with **9.** _____ pounds. He wants to open an account. He is suggested to open a Higher Rate Deposit Account which requires **10.** _____ to open the account. Its interests is **11.** _____ on net and **12.** _____ on gross.

13. A Higher Rate Deposit Account is calculated daily. (   )

14. He can get a special card to his cash money. (   )

15. The rate of interest will go down to 5.52% if the savings go below five hundred pounds. (   )

16. The Higher Rate Deposit Account allows people to be five hundred pounds overdrawn. (   )

③ Activity Three

Direction: In this section, you will hear two long conversations. At the end of the first conversation, you will be given 15 seconds to answer the questions. At the end of the second conversation, you will be given 10 seconds to answer the questions.

Conversation One

17. A. He's taking a break from studying.

   B. He has already finished studying.

   C. He was assigned to watch a program by his professor.

   D. He's finding out some information for a friend.

18. A. She did poorly on a recent test.

   B. She thinks the man have studied the linear algebra well.

   C. She thinks they may study more efficiently if they work together.

   D. She wants to help the man with his linear algebra.

19. A. He and Elizabeth argued recently.

   B. He doesn't want to bother Elizabeth so late in the evening.

   C. He heard Elizabeth did poorly on the last test.

   D. He'd rather study in his own dormitory.

Conversation Two

20. A. He wants to become a cook.

    B. He hopes to go on to graduate school.

    C. He wants to travel around the world.

    D. He'd like to work at a hotel.

21. A. At a bakery.   **B.** In a library.

    C. At a restaurant.   **D.** At a travel agency.

④ Activity Four

*Direction: In this section, you will hear a passage **THREE TIMES**. When the passage is read for the first time, you should listen carefully for its general idea. When the passage is read for the second time, you are required to fill in the blanks with the exact words you have just heard. Finally, when the passage is read for the third time, you should check what you have written.*

The first copyright law in the United States was passed by Congress in 1790. In 1976 Congress enacted the latest copyright law, **22.** _____ the technological developments that had occurred since the passage of the Copyright Act of 1909. For example, in 1909, anyone who wanted to make a single copy of a **23.** _____ work for personal use had to do so by hand. The very process **24.** _____ a limitation on the quantity of materials copied. Today, a photocopier can do the work in seconds; the limitation has disappeared. The 1909 law did not provide full protection for films and sound recording, nor did it **25.** _____ the need to protect radio and television. As a result, **26.** _____ of the law and abuses of the intent of the law have lessened the **27.** _____ rewards of authors, artists, and producers. The 1976 Copyright Act has not prevented these abuses fully, but it has clarified the legal rights of the injured parties and given them an **28.** _____ for remedy.

Since 1976 the Act has been **29.** _____ to include computer software, and guidelines have been adopted for fair use of television broadcasts. These changes have cleared up much of the confusion and conflict that followed **30.** _____ the 1976 legislation.

The fine points of the law are decided by the courts and by acceptable common practice over time. As these decisions and agreements are made, we modify our behavior accordingly. For now, we need to **31.** _____ the law and its guidelines as accurately as we can and to act in a fair manner.

Unit 7
Internet Addiction

Learning Objectives

- To learn expressions of describing the bad effects of Internet addiction
- To learn to guess main ideas according to questions or your own knowledge
- To learn to listen for implied meanings
- To learn skills of giving a persuasive speech on a question of value

Section A Listening

Pre-Listening

Direction: Work in pairs and discuss the following questions.

1. What is Internet addiction in your opinion?
2. What are the warning signs of Internet addiction?

Warm-up Activities

⚙ Vocabulary

deter	[dɪ'tɜ˞]	*vt.*	try to prevent; show opposition to 阻止；制止
sensitive	['sensətɪv]	*adj.*	being susceptible to the attitudes, feelings, or circumstances of others 敏感的
peak	[pik]	*n.*	the top point of a mountain or hill 山峰；最高点
maturation	[ˌmætʃʊ'reʃn]	*n.*	coming to full development; becoming mature 成熟
customize	['kʌstəmaɪz]	*vt.*	make to specifications 定制，定做
outcast	['aʊtkæst]	*n.*	a person who is rejected (from society or home) 被抛弃者
sedentary	['sednterɪ]	*adj.*	requiring sitting or little activity 需要坐着的
ominous	['ɑmɪnəs]	*adj.*	suggesting that something bad is about to happen; threatening 不祥的，坏兆头的
tailored	['telə˞d]	*adj.*	made or done specially for someone's particular need or situation 定做的
misrepresent	[ˌmɪsˌreprɪ'zent]	*vt.*	represent falsely 歪曲
marijuana	[ˌmærə'wɑnə]	*n.*	a drug which is made from the dried leaves and flowers of the hemp plant, and which can be smoked 大麻
recoil	[rɪ'kɔɪl]	*vi.*	draw oneself back in fear, digust, etc.（因恐惧、厌恶等）畏缩，退缩

stunt	[stʌnt]	*vt.*	prevent the growth or development of 阻碍……发育（生长）
conducive	[kənˈdusɪv]	*adj.*	tending to bring about; being partly responsible for 有助于……的
trump	[trʌmp]	*vt.*	get the better of 胜过

① Activity One

Direction: In this section, you will hear the first part of a passage. After listening, you should decide whether the following statements are true (T) or false (F). Now listen to the passage.

1. Human curiosity is perhaps at its peak during one's teenage years. (   )

2. Talking to your teen about these sensitive subjects before he or she has a chance to search online can be a great way to remove his or her need to surf the web for more information. (   )

3. The Internet is capable of knowing who is using it at any given time and how to customize its settings. (   )

② Activity Two

Direction: Listen to the rest of the passage and decide whether the following statements are true (T) or false (F).

4. Getting outside, going to social gatherings, and just having a good time with friends are the most productive and satisfying activities in which teenagers can engage. (   )

5. Social networks and online gaming are substitutes for real life. (   )

6. Parents should limit the time that their teens are allowed to spend on school projects and some degree of entertainment. (   )

While-Listening

Text A For a Restful Night, Make Your Smart Phone Sleep on the Couch

⚙ Vocabulary

banish	['bænɪʃ]	*vt.*	drive away 放逐，驱逐
roam	[rom]	*vi.*	move about aimlessly or without any destination, often in search of food or employment 漫游；漫步
insomnia	[ɪn'sɑmnɪə]	*n.*	an inability to sleep; chronic sleeplessness 失眠症
chronic	['krɑnɪk]	*adj.*	being long-lasting and recurrent or characterized by long suffering 慢性的；长期的
exacerbate	[ɪg'zæsɚbet]	*vt.*	make worse 使恶化；使加重
hallmark	['hɔlmɑrk]	*n.*	a distinctive characteristic or attribute 特点；标志
intrusion	[ɪn'truʒn]	*n.*	entrance by force or without permission or welcome 闯入；打扰
gadget	['gædʒɪt]	*n.*	a device or control that is very useful for a particular job 小工具；小装置

❶ Activity One

Direction: In this section, you will hear a long passage. After listening, you should choose the best answer to each question. Now listen to the passage.

1. What is the author's $7 solution?

   A. An old-fashioned watch.   **B.** An old-fashioned alarm clock.

   C. An old-fashioned computer.   **D.** An old-fashioned TV.

2. According to Dr. Claman, what is becoming a more common contributing factor of insomnia for people in their 20s and 30s?

   A. The alarm clock.   **B.** The noise.

   C. The phone.   **D.** The pressure.

3. According to the National Center on Sleep Disorders Research at the National Institutes of Health, how many Americans have chronic insomnia?

    A. 10%–15%.   **B.** 20%–30%.

    C. 30%–40%.   **D.** 40%–50%.

4. According to the 2013 Facebook-sponsored study by IDC Research, how many people who own a smart phone said they use it as an alarm clock?

    A. 18%.   **B.** 24%.   **C.** 44%.   **D.** 54%.

5. The phone in the bedroom could set off what Orfeu M. Buxton called "threat vigilance", then what is **NOT** true about it?

    A. It is a type of excessive light that keeps you awake.

    B. It means that you're never off.

    C. It means you're always watchful.

    D. It is a hallmark to insomnia.

❷ Activity Two

Direction: Listen again and decide whether the following statements are true (T) or false (F).

6. According to sleep researchers, flipping your phone to quiet mode isn't good for you to have a good sleep. (   )

7. According to the National Center on Sleep Disorders Research at the National Institutes of Health, as many as 40 percent of Americans suffer from chronic insomnia in a given year. (   )

8. Most new alarm clocks connected with smart phones help people sleep well. (   )

9. According to Mr. Buxton, 10 percent of teens in middle school are hardened insomniacs. (   )

10. Now the speaker takes no electronics in his bedroom. (   )

Text B Screen Addiction Is Taking a Toll on Children

⚙ Vocabulary

documentary	[ˌdɑkjə'mɛntrɪ]	*n.*	a film or TV program presenting the facts about a person or event 纪录片
junkie	['dʒʌŋkɪ]	*n.*	a narcotics addict 吸毒者；爱好者
clinical	['klɪnɪkl]	*adj.*	relating to a clinic or conducted in or as if in a clinic and depending on direct observation of patients 临床的
afflict	[ə'flɪkt]	*vt.*	cause pain or suffering in 折磨；使受痛苦
adept	[ə'dɛpt]	*adj.*	having or showing knowledge and skill and aptitude 精于……的，擅长……的
therapy	['θɛrəpɪ]	*n.*	(medicine) the act of caring for someone (as by medication or remedial training, etc.) 治疗；疗法
pediatrics	[ˌpidɪ'ætrɪks]	*n.*	the branch of medicine concerned with the treatment of infants and children 儿科
soothe	[suð]	*vt.*	cause to feel better 安慰；缓和
infringe	[ɪn'frɪndʒ]	*vi.*	interfere with (sth); violate 干涉；干扰
epidemic	[ˌɛpɪ'dɛmɪk]	*adj.*	prevalent among people 流行的

① Activity One

Direction: In this section, you will hear a long passage. After listening, you should decide whether the following statements are true (T) or false (F). Now listen to the passage.

1. Chinese doctors say the therapy has been proved effective. (   )

2. Internet addiction has been considered a clinical diagnosis. (   )

3. According to a Kaiser Family Foundation study in 2010, older children and teenagers spend more than 8 hours per day with a variety of different media. (   )

4. According to a Kaiser Family Foundation study in 2010, television remains the dominant medium. (   )

5. The academy stated two-thirds of those questioned in the Kaiser study said their parents had some rules about how much time the youngsters spent with media. (   )

❷ Activity Two

Direction: Listen again and answer the following questions.

6. According to a Kaiser Family Foundation study in 2010, how many hours do older children and teenagers spend per day with a variety of different media?

7. Why are parents grateful for electronics?

8. Why does the pediatrics academy maintain that children should not be exposed to any electronic media before age 2?

9. On average, how many texts do teenagers send a night after they get into bed according to an earlier Pew study?

10. According to Ms. Hatch, why do children begin to feel more lonely and depressed?

Post-Listening

Direction: Work in pairs and discuss the following questions.

1. What are the effects of Internet addiction?
2. How to avoid Internet addiction?

Section B Speaking

Persuasion on a Question of Value

Persuasive speeches are intended to put across a point to the audience or to convince the audience to do something. It is the art of presenting an argument with clarity and impact. Persuasive speeches are an effective way to appeal to both the mind and heart of the audience, thus achieving the purpose of influencing and persuading the audience.

When you give a persuasive speech on a question of value, you are basically talking about "Is it good or is it bad? Moral or immoral? Just or unjust?" In other words, you are making fundamental value judgments concerning what is right or wrong. Your task is to convince the audience of what you think is right and seek intellectual agreement from them. A successful persuasive speech on questions of value can often influence or even change audience's opinion about significant issues. However, you are not asking listeners to do anything.

It is important to realize that questions of value are a lot more than matters of personal preferences or personal opinions. You cannot make and support a claim on a question of value simply because you like it or you think it is cool. What you need to do is justify your statement—to state the facts, statistics and reasons that will back up your claim.

In planning a persuasive speech on a question of value, the following steps are essential:

First, it is essential to understand the topic. Some fundamental value questions, such as Internet addiction, human cloning, race relations, and violence on TV are very complicated issues and you need to make sure you know what they are about before you can talk intelligently and responsibly about them.

Then it is essential to take a definite stand and stay committed to it. An effective persuasion should make a definite point, and urge the listeners to adopt a certain position or belief. A definite stand does not mean an absolute point. In this sense, an either-or point is much more valued than a both-and point. Yet Chinese students are quite often afraid of committing themselves to a clear-cut point. They try to "stay in the middle" to avoid a strong, clear point. This is not a good habit. Being ambiguous and vague is no way of avoiding being absolute; it will instead damage your credibility.

Also, you need to decide on your position statement. Your position statement states your definite point, which is to be supported with related points and materials. A statement of value indicates that you will present arguments, facts and evidence to persuade the audience that something is good, just, wise, and so on. Your position statement covers the controlling idea of the whole speech, yet it should also be specific enough to state the exact opinion.

In order to effectively prove or support your point, you need to do research work to find and select the best supporting materials. Your supporting materials and evidence may include expert opinion, statistics, factual instances, personal experiences, and so on. In order to obtain a variety of apt, effective evidence, doing research is a must. You'd better use a variety of evidence to support your point rather than build your argument on one example or one isolated incident.

Now comes the task of organizing your speech and working out your major supporting points. You can prepare an outline of main points and needed information and evidence. A sample is given below:

Speech Outline

Topic: *Human cloning*

Purpose: *To persuade the audience that human cloning is ethically unsound and technically risky*

Position statement:

Due to the inefficiency and uncertainty of animal cloning and the lack of understanding about reproductive cloning, it would be highly unethical and risky to attempt to clone humans at this point of time.

Main points:

1. The success rate of animal cloning is only about 1 or 2 viable offsprings for every 100 experiments.

2. About 30% of clones born alive are affected with "large-offspring syndrome".

3. There are still many unknowns concerning reproductive cloning.

4. Scientists do not know how cloning could impact mental development.

Conclusion:

Although it may raise hopes for new treatments, human cloning, particularly human reproductive cloning, should be approached with great caution and care.

Once you have all the points and evidence in place, you can go on to compose and then rehearse the speech. While composing the speech, do not forget to design a forceful beginning and ending for your speech. In delivery, try to establish your credibility and trustworthiness through controlling your vocal quality and maintaining eye contact.

Questions to Think About

1. What is the difference between an absolute point and a definite point? Discuss with your classmates and give examples to illustrate the differences.

2. Apart from expert opinion, statistics, factual instances and personal experiences, what other evidence can you use to support a point?

3. Study the following statements and decide which ones are effective position statements.

   (1) There are many movies about friendships.

   (2) Women are lousy drivers.

   (3) Movies about men's friendships earn more money than movies about women's friendships.

(4) I believe there's no point judging students' achievement based on the scores of a standard test.

(5) Women always have close friendships, but men seldom do.

(6) Although people spend more time at work than almost anywhere else, the dangers and risks of office romance are quite high, too.

(7) Internet forums are not as effective as it is believed as an indicator of public opinion.

(8) Given the present situation in the entertainment market, big-budget movies represent the best future for the Chinese movie industry.

Communication Tasks

1. Choose one of the following topics and try to decide on your stand. Then compose your position statement to state your stand to your classmates.

   (1) Children's Internet addiction and parenting style

   (2) Internet addiction in adults

   (3) Unlicensed software

   (4) Friendship in the era of social networking

   (5) Stress suffered by IT professionals

   (6) Women leaders in today's world

2. Now do research work to find materials and evidence to support the stand you choose in the previous task, and work out a speech outline including your stand, your main points, and your evidence.

3. Compose the speech following your outline. Rehearse it and delivery it to your classmates.

Section C Exam Spotlight

Activity One

*Direction: In this section, you will hear three news reports **ONLY ONCE**. At the end of each news report, you will be given 10 seconds to answer the questions.*

News Item One

1. **A.** Portugal.   **B.** Costa Rica.   **C.** Morocco.   **D.** Australia.

2. **A.** In 1956.   **B.** In 1960.   **C.** In 1964.   **D.** In 1968.

News Item Two

3. **A.** A violent hurricane.   **B.** Far away from home.

   C. Good academic reputation.   **D.** Money-back guarantee.

4. **A.** Heavy rains haven't struck Queensland for a long time.

   B. People in Queensland have done some preparation for it.

   C. There was no reports about people's missing or injury.

   D. The bad weather may be tough for couples.

News Item Three

5. **A.** In America.   **B.** In Canada.   **C.** In Haiti.   **D.** In Great Britain.

6. **A.** 100,000.   **B.** 500,000.   **C.** 150,000.   **D.** 510,000.

② Activity Two

*Direction: In this section, you will hear a passage **THREE TIMES**. When the passage is read for the first time, you should listen carefully for its general idea. When the passage is read for the second time, you are required to fill in the blanks either with the exact words you have just heard or the main points in your own words. Finally, when the passage is read for the third time, you should check what you have written.*

A couple of months ago, I went to a department store to buy a few things for the house. I needed a set of curtains for the living room, two table lamps, a rug and several **7.** _____. I asked them to **8.** _____ the things as soon as possible, but they said that they were unable to send them out until 20 days later. After about 3 weeks, I received only the curtains and lamps. I was a little disappointed when I didn't receive all the **9.** _____ I had bought. But nevertheless, I was eager to see what the curtains and lamps looked like. I first opened the **10.** _____ with curtains. I had bought a lovely **11.** _____ blue, and instead they had sent me a horrible dark **12.** _____. Well, you can just **13.** _____ how angry I was. Then I opened the boxes with the lamps.

They were exactly what I'd **14.** _____. But one of the lamp's shape was damaged.

15. _____. They promised to come and

16. _____. It has been two weeks since my

complaint. **17.** _____.

---

③ Activity Three

Direction: In this section, you will hear two long conversations. At the end of each conversation, you will be given 15 seconds to answer the questions.

Conversation One

18. A. The network.   **B.** The market.   **C.** The factory.   **D.** The company.

19. A. Business executives.   **B.** White-collar workers.

     C. College students.   **D.** Office ladies.

20. A. Fierce competition.   **B.** Network problems.

     C. High price.   **D.** Government policy.

Conversation Two

21. A. Examples of different types of children.

     B. How to run parenting workshops.

     C. The way to communicate with children.

     D. The way to control children.

22. A. On no occasion.   **B.** On rare, important occasions.

     C. On every occasion.   **D.** On not-so-important occasions.

23. A. They see it as encouragement.   **B.** They see it as a challenge.

     C. They see it as a danger.   **D.** They see it as a risk.

④ Activity Four

*Direction: In this section, you will hear a passage **ONLY ONCE**. After listening, you should fill in the blanks. Now listen to the passage.*

Reading

Nowadays few of us read books after we leave school. This is rather **24.** _____ , for one should know that books are no less necessary to one's **25.** _____ life than fresh air is to one's **26.** _____ life. From good reading we can derive **27.** _____ , experience and **28.** _____ . A good book is our **29.** _____ friend. It can increase our contentment when we are **30.** _____ and happy, and lessen our pain when we are sad or lonely. Books can also offer us a wide range of experience. Few of us can travel far from home or live long over 100, but all of us can live many lives through the pages of books. What's more, reading books can increase our **31.** _____ ability, **32.** _____ our minds and make us wise.

With the coming of TV, books are no longer read as widely as they once were. However, nothing can **33.** _____ the role that books play in our lives.

Unit 8
Online Learning

Learning Objectives

- To get to know more resources of learning
- To learn how to make use of open online courses
- To learn some types of the flipped classroom
- To learn to introduce the main speaker

Section A Listening

Pre-Listening

Direction: Work in pairs and discuss the following questions.

1. What are the differences between open online courses and courses in classrooms?

2. If you were a teacher, how will you teach your students?

Warm-up Activities

⚙ Vocabulary

deserted	[dɪˈzɜːtɪd]	*adj.*	remote from civilization 荒芜的；被遗弃的
unattended	[ˌʌnəˈtɛndɪd]	*adj.*	left alone without anyone in charge 没人照顾的；未被注意的
subtractive	[səbˈtræktɪv]	*adj.*	able or tending to remove or subtract 可减去的；负的
lathe	[leð]	*n.*	a machine that shapes wood or metal, by turning it around and around against a sharp tool 车床；机床
mill	[mɪl]	*vt.*	grind something such as coffee beans or pepper into powder 碾磨
customized	[ˈkʌstəmaɪzd]	*adj.*	made according to the specifications of an individual 定制的；用户化的

❶ Activity One

Direction: In this section, you will hear a short passage. After listening, you should choose the best answer to each question. Now listen to the passage.

1. How many machines are there in the small factory?

   A. Eighteen. **B.** Sixteen.

   C. Eight. **D.** Ten.

2. Why does the factory appear deserted?

   A. Because the factory will go into liquidation.

   B. Because there is no enough money for the factory to refine its appearance.

   C. Because additive-manufacturing machines are put into use.

   D. Because most of the employees left the factory.

3. What is 3D printing excellent for?

   A. Customized jobs.   **B.** Short production runs.

   C. Making prototypes.   **D.** All of the above.

Activity Two

Direction: Listen again and decide whether the following statements are true (T) or false (F).

4. Three-dimensional printers can run unattended day and night, seven days a week. (   )

5. The ink will be sintered by the printer into place with a laser in a way that creates little waste. (   )

6. There is no need to alter the software when the specification changes. (   )

While-Listening

Text A Resources for Free Online Learning

Vocabulary

treasure trove		*n.*	valuable things that are found hidden and whose owner is unknown 无主珍宝
compelling	[kəm'pɛlɪŋ]	*adj.*	very interesting or exciting, so that you have to pay attention 引人注目的
sample	['sæmpl]	*n.*	a small part or amount of something that is examined in order to find out something about the whole 样品；样本；例子

① Activity One

Direction: In this section, you will hear a passage. After listening, you should choose the best answer to each question. Now listen to the passage.

1. Which of the following form is **NOT** mentioned in Coursera?

   A. Discussion forums.   **B.** Interactive lessons.

   C. Quizzes.   **D.** Lectures.

2. In which case can Khan Academy be a right resource?

   A. Learning how to write the code.   **B.** Picking up a new language.

   C. Learning about a topic in short bursts. **D.** Getting to know more about science.

3. What will you choose if you're a user of iPad and iPhone?

   A. EdX.   **B.** MIT.

   C. Apple app.   **D.** iTunes U.

4. According to this passage, which is **NOT** the most useful language to develop interactive websites?

   A. HTML.   **B.** Python.

   C. EdX.   **D.** PHP.

5. What are the more suitable tools for people who want to learn foreign languages?

   A. Livemocha and EdX.   **B.** Coursera and Duolingo.

   C. iTunes and MIT OpenCourseWare.   **D.** Duolingo and Livemocha.

② Activity Two

Direction: Listen again and decide whether the following statements are true (T) or false (F).

6. All these eight websites are free and can be used at home for people with a web browser and an Internet connection. (   )

7. Khan Academy will provide certificates of completion to prove that you passed the class. (   )

8. Massachusetts Institute of Technology does well especially in science, computer and engineering. (   )

9. Course materials of EdX come from a number of universities, such as Harvard, University of Hong Kong. (   )

10. You should communicate with native speakers for the purpose of learning a new language in Duolingo. (   )

Text B Models of the Flipped Classroom

⚙ Vocabulary

flipped classroom		*n.*	a form of blended learning in which students learn content online by watching video lectures, usually at home, and homework is done in class with teachers and students discussing and solving questions 翻转课堂
synthesize	['sɪnθəsaɪz]	*vt.*	make something by combining different things or substances 合成；综合
implement	['ɪmplɪmɛnt]	*vt.*	take action or make changes to make what you have officially decided happen 实施，执行；实现，使生效
slide	[slaɪd]	*n.*	a small piece of film in a frame that you shine a light through to show a picture on a screen or wall 幻灯片
worksheet	['wɜkʃit]	*n.*	a piece of paper with questions and exercises for students（学生的）活页练习题
handheld	[hændhɛld]	*adj.*	small and light enough to be operated while you hold it in your hands 掌上型的；手持型的
anonymously	[ə'nɑnəməslɪ]	*adv.*	without giving a name 匿名地；化名地
fraction	['frækʃən]	*n.*	a small part or item forming a piece of a whole 部分；小部分

① Activity One

Direction: In this section, you will hear a short passage. After listening, you should choose the best answer to each question. Now listen to the passage.

1. Which subject is **NOT** mentioned when the flipped classroom was applied to demonstrate its broad practicability?

A. Physics.   B. Geography.

C. History.   D. Biology.

2. Which is **NOT** the tool provided for students in an inverted classroom to gain first exposure to material outside of class?

A. Textbook readings.   B. Lecture videos.

C. After class self-test exercises. D. Powerpoint presentations with voice-over.

3. What is the class time structured around in peer instruction?

A. Small group discussions.   B. Mini-lectures.

C. Conceptual questions.   D. Both B and C.

4. According to this passage, which is **NOT** one of the models of the flipped classroom?

A. Peer Instruction model.   B. Assignment-based model.

C. Teacher-Student interaction model. D. Inverted classroom.

② Activity Two

Direction: Listen again and decide whether the following statements are true (T) or false (F).

5. The flipped classroom is a newly-developed teaching method, which has not been used in scientific disciplines. (   )

6. Walvoord and Anderson proposed a model where students gain first-exposure learning after class. (   )

7. Students will receive more extensive written feedback from the instructor through the processing activities which occur during class. (   )

8. Lage, Platt, and Treglia reported the application of a similar approach as the inverted classroom in an introductory economics course in 2000. (   )

9. Instructors found that students appeared more motivated when the course was taught in an inverted classroom. (   )

10. If 45% students of the whole class answer incorrectly, the instructors will circulate to promote productive discussions. (   )

Post-Listening

Direction: Work in pairs and discuss the following questions.

1. List some apps you often use when learning foreign languages and give a brief introduction about how they help you.

2. What do you think about the present teaching model?

Introducing the Main Speaker

At meetings, conferences or seminars, very often you may need to make a speech of introduction for the purpose of introducing the main speaker. A good introduction should capture the audience's attention, bring them together as a group and motivate them to listen attentively to the speaker.

As the introducer, you need to make sure that the main speaker will get the welcome he or she deserves. Your speech of introduction should be simple, positive and to the point. Usually a speech of introduction has the following 3 parts: **an opening** that grabs the audience's attention, **a body** that tells the audience something about the speaker and the topic, and **a closing** that welcomes the speaker to the stage.

The opening should make your audience sit up and take notice. You need to know about your audience's interests and concerns before you make the speech. For example, if you are talking to accountants, an amazing financial fact should jerk them awake, whereas it probably would not raise an eyebrow for an audience of fire-fighters. So do some research and understand your audience before you decide what to say.

The body part of your introduction should be able to maintain your audience interest in the main speaker and built up their anticipation of the following speech. So you need to relate to information and details that can establish credibility of the main speaker. Credibility topics may include the main speaker's achievements, awards, publications, media interest, qualifications, experience or other personal details that may do credit to the speaker.

The closing should be a warm and sincere welcome to the speaker. By say something like "so let's welcome to the stage Professor Jessie Martin", you hand the stage over to the main speaker smoothly with enthusiasm. Make sure that the final words of your introduction should be the name of the guest speaker. Know the speaker's name and how to pronounce it correctly.

Also remember that an introduction usually should not be longer than three minutes, so choose the most effective details about the speaker you are introducing. Do not give your own speech on the topic which the main speaker will be covering because the audience wants to hear the speaker, not the introducer.

Questions to Think About

1. What should be the focus of a speech given to introduce the main speaker?

2. Why is it important to do audience analysis before giving the speech? How would the audience's interests and concerns influence what you should say?

3. Suppose you are going to introduce 1) a university professor, 2) a sales manager, 3) a director of an E-learning center as the main speaker, what would be the appropriate credibility topics and details you would use for each of them in your speech?

Communication Tasks

1. What is your favorite TED speech? Who is the speaker? Do research work about the speaker and find out about his/her achievements, credentials and interesting personal information.

2. Based on your findings in task 1, compose a 2-minute mini-speech introducing the speaker to your class.

3. Deliver a short speech of introduction to introduce a not so well-known singer, actor, artist or writer to your classmates. You need to research into this person's career and life, and decide on what details to use in your introduction so as to enhance his/her credibility and reputation.

Section  Exam Spotlight

❶ Activity One

*Direction: In this section, you will hear three news reports **ONLY ONCE**. At the end of each news report, you will be given 10 seconds to answer the questions.*

News Item One

1. **A.** A U.S. company and a U.K. company.

   B. A Swiss company and a U.K. company.

   C. Two companies in Taiwan, China.

   D. A Chinese mainland company and a U.S. company.

2. **A.** Unilever.   **B.** Nestle.   **C.** Pepsi Co.   **D.** Coca Cola.

News Item Two

3. **A.** The economic recession.   **B.** The GDP of Singapore.

   C. The depressed export demand.   **D.** The production decline.

4. **A.** 6.   **B.** 12.   **C.** 9.   **D.** 5.

News Item Three

5. **A.** By restoring the degraded forests.   **B.** By reducing carbon's harmful effects.

   C. By improving the environment.   **D.** By creating millions of green jobs.

6. **A.** It is on the state of the world environment.

   B. It is to be released on March 16th.

   C. It tackles the economic downturn.

   D. It comes ahead of World Forest Week.

② Activity Two

Direction: In this section, you will hear a university lecturer giving a lecture about fast food consumption in a class. Look at the bar chart below and write the correct country to each blank.

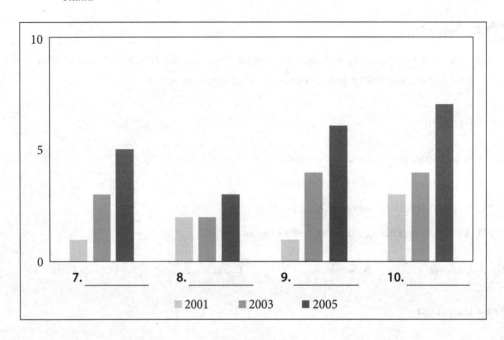

7. _____ 8. _____ 9. _____ 10. _____

■ 2001 ■ 2003 ■ 2005

③ Activity Three

Direction: Listen again and match the major health problems with the age groups below by ticking (✓) the relevant boxes in each column.

		Diabetes	Heart Disease	Asthma	Poor Brain Function
11.	16–24 years old				
12.	25–34 years old				
13.	35–44 years old				
14.	45–54 years old				
15.	55–64 years old				
16.	65+ years old				

④ Activity Four

Direction: In this section, you will hear a conversation about the meal ticket problem. After listening, you should choose the best answer(s) to each question. Now listen to the conversation.

17. **A.** He lost his meal card.   **B.** He wanted to change his meal plan.

    C. He had no more meals left on his card.   **D.** He didn't like the food in the cafeteria.

18. **A.** An error was made with the student's meal plan.

    B. The student forgot to pay his meal free.

    C. The student tried to use the wrong card.

    D. The student didn't renew his meal card.

19. **A.** She gave him proof of payment.   **B.** She allowed him to cancel his meal plan.

    C. She replaced his meal card.   **D.** She upgraded his meal plan.

20. **(Choose Two Answers)**

    A. Cash.   **B.** Credit.

    C. A revised receipt.   **D.** An updated bill.

⑤ Activity Five

Direction: Listen again to a part of the conversation and choose the best answer to the question.

21. **A.** He is not sure the problem has been solved.

    B. He is afraid he was overcharged.

    C. He might want to make another change.

    D. He forgot how many meals he ordered.

⑥ Activity Six

*Direction: In this section, you will hear a conversation **ONLY ONCE**. While listening, you may write **NO MORE THAN THREE WORDS** for each gap. Now listen to the conversation.*

M: Today my guest is Dana Ivanovich who has worked for the last twenty years as an interpreter. Dana, welcome.

W: Thank you.

M: Now I'd like to begin by saying that I have on occasions used an interpreter myself, as a **22.** _____, so I am full of admiration for what you do. But I think your profession is sometimes **23.** _____, and many people think anyone who speaks more than one language can do it.

W: There aren't any interpreters I know who don't have **24.** _____ and training. You only really get **25.** _____ after many years in the job.

M: And am I right in saying you can divide what you do into two distinct methods, simultaneous and consecutive interpreting?

W: That's right. The techniques you use are different, and a lot of interpreters will say one is easier than the other, less stressful.

M: Simultaneous interpreting, putting someone's words into another language **26.** _____ _____ as they speak, sounds to me like the more difficult.

W: Well, actually no, most people in the business would agree that consecutive interpreting is the more stressful. You have to wait for the speaker to deliver quite **27.** _____ language, before you then put it into the second language, which puts your short-term memory under **28.** _____.

M: You make notes, I presume.

W: Absolutely, anything like numbers, names, places, have to be noted down, but the rest is never translated word for word. You have to find a way of summarizing it so that the message is there. Turning every single word into the **29.** _____ would put too much strain on the interpreters and slow down the whole process too much.

M: But with simultaneous interpreting, you start translating almost as soon as the other person starts speaking. You must have some preparation beforehand.

W: Well, hopefully the speakers will let you have an outline of the topic a day or two in advance. You have a little time to do research, prepare **30.** _____ and so on.

Unit 9
Internet Economy

Learning Objectives

- To learn the development about the Internet economy
- To learn the skill of writing down English numbers
- To learn to find useful information from the material
- To learn skills of presenting an award

Section A Listening

Pre-Listening

Direction: Work in pairs and discuss the following questions.

1. Do you know any online celebrity? Could you introduce him/her to us briefly?

2. Why could the online celebrity be popular?

Warm-up Activities

⚙ Vocabulary

spurt	[spɜ·t]	*n.*	sudden burst of speed, effort, activity, etc. 突然的加速；劲头的迸发；活跃程度的突然加大
copper	[ˈkɑpɚ]	*n.*	Copper is reddish brown metal that is used to make things such as coins and electrical wires. 铜

① Activity One

Direction: In this section, you will hear a passage. After listening, you should choose the best answer to each question. Now listen to the passage.

1. According to the passage, what is the value of the web economy in G20 countries by 2016?

    A. $2.3 trillion.　　　　　　　**B.** £1.5 trillion.

    C. $4.2 trillion.　　　　　　　**D.** £2.6 trillion.

2. According to the study, how many people will be using the Internet in four years?

    A. 3 billion people.

    B. 2 billion people.

    C. More than 50% of the world's population.

    D. Less than 50% of the world's population.

3. In the future, what's the trend related to traditional Internet access?

    A. It will be more popular.

    B. It will not change.

    C. It will be used by less people.

    D. It is a kind of Internet access via a copper wire and a desktop PC.

4. According to the passage, what does the rapid fall in the cost of smart phones mean?

    A. It means cheap versions.

    B. It means 80% of all Internet users will access the web using a mobile phone by 2016.

    C. It means little people use the smart phones.

    D. It means more people use the smart phones

5. In 2010, what was the value of the Internet economy in the G20 group of leading nations?

    A. It was larger than the economies of Italy and Brazil.

    B. It accounted for 4.1% of the total size of world economies.

    C. It was larger than the economies of Israel and Brazil.

    D. It was worth $2.3 trillion.

While-Listening

Text A China's Internet Celebrity Economy

⚙ Vocabulary

allegedly	[əˈlɛdʒɪdlɪ]	*adv.*	according to what has been alleged 据说，据称
roughly	[ˈrʌflɪ]	*adv.*	imprecise but fairly close to correct 粗略地；大概地
derisively	[dɪˈraɪsɪvlɪ]	*adv.*	in a disrespectful and mocking manner 嘲弄地；嘲笑地
counterpart	[ˈkaʊntəpɑːt]	*n.*	a person or thing having the same function or characteristics as another 极相似的人或物
drastically	[ˈdræstɪkəlɪ]	*adv.*	in a drastic manner 彻底地；激烈地；大幅度地

1 Activity One

Direction: In this section, you will hear a long passage. After listening, you should choose the best answer to each question. Now listen to the passage.

1. What is the reason that Zhu Chenhui has become famous recently?

   A. Because she is the girlfriend of China's "No.1 eligible bachelor" Wang Sicong.

   B. Because of further gossip with other people.

   C. Because she would make around 150 million yuan this year.

   D. Because she is beautiful.

2. Which of the following statements could **NOT** be used for describing "Wang Hong"?

   A. Some of them have similar features of a tiny face, sharp chin, extraordinarily big eyes.

   B. They are often suggested to have had cosmetic surgery in South Korea.

   C. Many of them have turned their good looks and online fame into money.

   D. They all have online shop on Taobao.

3. Which of the following is **CORRECT** about Zhang Dayi?

   A. She is a model of fashion magazines now.

   B. She is the owner of an online shop that is set up on Taobao.

   C. She has more than 4 million fans on China's Sina Weibo.

   D. She designed the clothes for her fans.

4. According to the data from Taobao, how many shops are run by Internet celebrities?

   A. 5,000.   **B.** 2,014.

   C. 1,000.   **D.** 500,000.

5. How do web celebrities reduce the costs of their online shops in the supply chain?

   A. They have a huge fan base on social media.

   B. They can turn their popularity into productivity.

   C. They post photos of their new clothes first and then decide how many to produce based on the online comments.

   D. They launch a small number of products and then determine whether to promote them or not depending on initial market response.

② Activity Two

Direction: Listen again and decide whether the following statements are true (T) or false (F).

6. Zhu Chenhui could earn 128 million yuan a year, which is more than Fan Bingbing, China's richest celebrity. (　　)

7. All of the new products of the online store run by Zhang Dayi were sold out in three days, which is equivalent to the sales volume of a brick-and-mortar shop over a one-year period. (　　)

8. Some women's clothing shops on Taobao are quite different from others, so they have turned into blogs, and their owners designed clothes independently. (　　)

9. Unlike some of their counterparts in Western countries, Chinese Internet celebrities have developed their own brands. (　　)

10. An Internet celebrity with 500,000 followers can easily make around 40,000 yuan. (　　)

Text B Change of Web Economy: The New Internet

⚙ Vocabulary

sensor	['sensər]	n.	any device that receives a signal or stimulus (as heat or pressure or light or motion, etc.) and responds to it in a distinctive manner 传感器
outperform	[ˌaʊtpərˈfɔrm]	vt.	be or do something to a greater degree 胜过；做得比……好
widget	['wɪdʒɪt]	n.	something unspecified whose name is either forgotten or not known 小机械；小部件

① Activity One

*Direction: In this section, you will hear a news report **ONLY ONCE**. While listening, you may write **NO MORE THAN THREE WORDS** for each gap. Make sure the word(s) you fill in is (are) both grammatically and semantically acceptable. Now listen to the news report.*

Change of Web Economy: The New Internet

A. The Boston Consulting Group researchers speak of the **1.** _____ of a "new Internet" where:

B. Web access will not be a **2.** _____ any more.

The majority of web users will live in **3.** _____.

About **4.** _____ of all Internet users will access the web from a mobile.

The Internet will go social, and allow customers and companies to **5.** _____ each other.

C. This trend will be **6.** _____ another huge technology shift that will

7. _____ change the nature of how to run a business—the rise of the so-called

8. " _____ ".

D. 9. _____ IBM estimates that by 2015, one trillion devices will be

10. _____.

② Activity Two

Direction: Listen again and choose the best answer to each question.

11. According to the news, how many people in China will use the Internet within the four years?

    A. 800 million.   **B.** 8 billion.

    C. 300 million.   **D.** 3 billion.

12. In the digital economy, what do the businesses have to do?

    A. Entrepreneurs have to embrace the web economy.

    B. Businesses have to adapt their people, processes and structures.

    C. Understanding the economic potential of the web should be an urgent priority for leaders.

    D. Entrepreneurs have to build a digital business.

13. According to the news, what did the research fail to do?

    A. To find the balance of employment between new digital companies and old-style businesses.

    B. To find which company will gain most from the rapid growth of the Internet.

    C. To find a way of measuring the Internet economy.

    D. To find the actual part of the digital economy.

14. Which of the following companies does **NOT** have the Internet ecosystems?

    A. Amazon.   **B.** Facebook.

    C. Baidu.   **D.** BCG.

Post-Listening

Direction: Work in pairs and discuss the following questions.

1. What do you think of the E-commerce?

2. China's State Council released an implementation plan for "Internet Plus", an initiative aimed at using the Internet and related technologies to spur the next stage of economic development. As a university student, how do you think of the Internet Plus?

Section **B** Speaking

Presenting an Award

Speeches of presentation are given when someone is publicly receiving a gift, an award, or some other form of public recognition. Usually such speeches are brief. Sometimes they may be no more than a mere announcement such as "And the winner of the...award this year is …", or they may be up to four or five minutes in length.

Presenting an award is a real honor that is irresistible to most people, yet a speech of presentation is not just about how happy and honored you feel to be a presenter. It takes some serious consideration as to what to say when presenting the award to the winner. The point of a speech of presentation is to acknowledge the achievements of the recipient. In other words, you need to tell the audience why the recipient is receiving the award by pointing out his or her excellence, contributions, achievements and so forth. There is no need to deal with everything the winner has ever done. Instead, focus on the achievements directly concerning the award, and talk about these achievements in a way that will make them meaningful and inspiring to the audience. Make sure that you do your homework and know clearly about the winner's extraordinary achievements. At the end of your speech, you call out the winners on stage, congratulate the winner and move out.

Depending on the audience and the occasion, you may also need to discuss two other matters in a speech of presentation. First, if the audience is not familiar with the award and why it is being given, you should explain briefly—or at least allude to—the purpose of the award. Second, if the award was won in a public competition and the audience knows who the losers are, you might take a moment to praise the losers as well.

Questions to Think About

1. Is it a good idea not to disclose the winner's name till the very end of the presentation speech? Why or why not?

2. Watch the video of an award ceremony, such as the Oscar or the Grammy Awards ceremony and pay special attention to the speeches of presentation made by the artists. Does any of the presentation speeches inspire you in any way?

3. Have you noticed any differences in the style of presentation speeches made by movie stars and musicians? What kind of style do you think would suit you best?

Communication Tasks

1. Work with your classmates and create an award that you think is meaningful. Use your imagination and be creative. Then make a mini-speech to briefly explain the purpose of the award.

2. Form groups of four or five people. Each group is to perform a ceremony with a series of awards to present: the best designer, the best salesperson, the best service, the best team player, etc. Each of the group members should pick one award, write and deliver a speech of presentation and present the award to a group member.

Section C Exam Spotlight

Activity One

*Direction: In this section, you will hear three news reports **ONLY ONCE**. At the end of each news report, you will be given 10 seconds to answer the questions.*

News Item One

1. **A.** The conflict between oil workers and the Indian government.

   B. The crippled Indian commerce.

C. The policies issued by the Indian government.

D. Labor standoff between workers and the Indian government.

2. **A.** Arresting some strikers.   **B.** Giving a pay-raise as required.

   C. Threats of unemployment.   **D.** Talking with the workers.

News Item Two

3. **A.** Michael Jackson earned a lot of money and was once a prisoner.

   B. Michael Jackson was the lead singer of "The Jackson Five".

   C. Michael Jackson's life was a lonely and excessive one.

   D. Michael Jackson's album is one of the best sellers.

4. **A.** Five.   **B.** Seven.   **C.** Nine.   **D.** Fifty.

News Item Three

5. **A.** *Kilometre Zero.*   **B.** *Match Point.*

   C. *Star Wars: Episode III—Revenge of the Sith.*   **D.** *Election.*

6. **A.** *Kilometre Zero.*   **B.** *Star Wars: Episode III—Revenge of the Sith.*

   C. *Election.*   **D.** *Match Point.*

---

② Activity Two

*Direction: In this section, you will hear a university lecturer giving a lecture to a group of students about the role of motivation in foreign language learning. Complete the sentences below. Write **NO MORE THAN THREE WORDS** for each answer.*

7. Integrative motivation occurs when learners are ready to integrate with the _____ _____ of the target language.

8. Instrumental motivation is most powerful in situations where learners _____ to interact with its members.

9. Early research indicated that integrative orientation was stronger than instrumental orientation in _____.

10. More recently, researchers have found that integrative motivation is _____
measures of achievement.

---

③ Activity Three

*Direction: Listen again and answer the questions below. Write **NO MORE THAN FOUR WORDS** for each answer.*

11. What do adult foreign language learners need in order to learn the target language?

_____

List **TWO** important factors in foreign language learning.

12. _____

13. _____

14. What is one of the effects of having personal motivation for some learners?

_____

List **TWO** factors that motivation is dependent on.

15. _____

16. _____

---

④ Activity Four

Direction: In this section, you will hear a conversation. After listening, you should choose the best answer(s) to each question.

17. A. Study something different.   **B.** Find a way to pay his own tuition.

   C. Transfer to another school.   **D.** Apply for a scholarship.

18. A. A scholarship.   **B.** A second major.

   C. A loan.   **D.** A suspension of studies.

19. A. Try to change his father's mind.

    B. Take two majors simultaneously.

    C. Work for a while to save some money.

    D. Transfer to a less expensive school.

20. (Choose Two Answers)

    A. It will take longer to graduate.

    B. It will cost more.

    C. It would allow less time for the student's main interest.

    D. It will affect the student's social life.

⑤ Activity Five

Direction: Listen again to a part of the conversation and choose the best answer to the question.

21. A. She thinks it is an easy problem to solve.

    B. Many other students have the same problem.

    C. The student has discussed a similar problem with her before.

    D. She had already guessed what the student's problem was.

⑥ Activity Six

*Direction: In this section, you will hear a passage **ONLY ONCE**. After listening, you should fill in the blanks. Now listen to the passage.*

People nowadays seem to have the sense that their time has become more **22.** _____ .

Compared with early generations, we spend more and more time working and have less and less free time to engage in **23.** _____ . But this premise turns out to be an **24.** _____ . The most **25.** _____ data from major Time Use Service suggests, if anything, Americans today have more free time than the **26.** _____ .

But why do we feel like time so **27.** _____? One problem is that time becomes more **28.** _____ and time becomes more worth money. In one study, people who were **29.** _____ to think about money before entering a cafe spent less time **30.** _____ the other patrons and more time working. Those who are thinking their time did reverse spending time **31.** _____ instead of working.

Unit 10
Big Data

Learning Objectives

- To know what big data is
- To learn the skill of blank filling
- To learn the skill of grasping information and ideas
- To learn the skill of analyzing or explaining a process

Section Ⓐ Listening

Pre-Listening

Direction: Work in pairs and discuss the following questions.

1. Have you heard the term big data? Where do you store your data in daily life?

2. Do you know what big data is? Could you give some application examples of big data?

Warm-up Activities

⚙ Vocabulary

term	[tɜːm]	*n.*	a word or expression used for some particular thing 术语
archaeologist	[ˌɑːkɪˈɑlədʒɪst]	*n.*	a person who studies ancient societies by examining what remains of their buildings, graves, tools, etc. 考古学家

❶ Activity One

*Direction: In this section, you will hear a passage **ONLY ONCE**. While listening, you may write **NO MORE THAN THREE WORDS** for each gap. Make sure the word(s) you fill in is (are) both grammatically and semantically acceptable. Now listen to the passage.*

A. Now, you probably all have heard the term big data. In fact, you're probably **1.** _____ hearing the term big data.

B. What we find is that when we have **2.** _____ of data, we can **3.** _____ do things that we couldn't do when we only had smaller amounts.

C. Big data is important, and big data is new, and when you think about it, the only way this planet is going to deal with **4.** _____ — to **5.** _____, supply them with medical care, supply them with energy, electricity, and to make sure they're not burnt to a crisp because of **6.** _____ — is because of the **7.** _____ data.

D. Let's think about what information looked like, **8.** _____ looked like in the past. In 1908, on the island of Crete archaeologists discovered a clay disc. Now, there's **9.** _____ on this disc, but we actually don't know what it means. It's a complete mystery, but the point is that this is what information used to look like 4,000 years ago. This is how society **10.** _____ information.

While-Listening

Text A Big Data Is Better Data

⚙ Vocabulary

carjacker	[ˈkɑrˈdʒækɚ]		A carjacker is someone who attacks and steals from people who are driving their own cars. 劫车者
render into			译成（某种语言）
feathery	[ˈfɛð(ə)rɪ]	*adj.*	If something is feathery, it has an edge divided into a lot of thin parts so that it looks soft. 柔软如羽毛的；生有羽毛的
quill	[kwɪl]	*n.*	A bird's quills are large, stiff feathers on its wings and tail. 大翎毛；羽茎
inkwell	[ˈɪŋkwɛl]	*n.*	a small well holding writing ink into which a pen can be dipped 墨水池
telecommunication	[ˌtɛlɪkəˌmʊnəˈkeʃən]	*n.*	systems used in transmitting messages over a distance electronically 电讯；[通信] 远程通信；无线电通讯
telltale	[ˈtɛltel]	*adj.*	showing that something exists or has happened 明显的
biopsy	[ˈbaɪɑpsɪ]	*n.*	the removal and examination of fluids or tissue from a patient's body in order to discover why they are ill 活组织检查；活组织切片检查；切片检查法
cancerous	[ˈkænsɚrəs]	*adj.*	relating to or affected with cancer 癌的；生癌的；像癌的

biochemistry	[baɪoˈkemɪstrɪ]	*n.*	the organic chemistry of compounds and processes occuring in organisms; the effort to understand biology within the context of chemistry 生物化学
automation	[ˌɔtəˈmeʃən]	*n.*	the act of implementing the control of equipment with advanced technology; usually involving electronic hardware 自动化；自动操作
microscope	[ˈmaɪkrəskop]	*n.*	magnifier of the image of small objects 显微镜
stakeholder	[ˈstekholdɚ]	*n.*	someone entrusted to hold the stakes for two or more persons betting against one another 利益相关者

① Activity One

Direction: In this section, you will hear a long passage. After listening, you should decide whether the following statements are true (T) or false (F). Now listen to the passage.

1. In modern society, we still need the discs to store information. (　　)

2. Files that Edward Snowden took from the National Security Agency are heavy. (　　)

3. The disc that's 4,000 years old doesn't store a lot of information, but the information is unchangeable. (　　)

4. Your location information could only be recorded with a cell phone that has a GPS. (　　)

5. With the help of big data, a non-approved driver could start the car. (　　)

② Activity Two

Direction: Listen again and choose the best answer to each question.

6. What is the difference between the information stored in the past and at present?

   A. We can store the same information as before.

   B. The information is heavier.

C. The information could be used easier.

D. The information could be saved longer than before.

7. According to the passage, which of the following statements is the value of big data?

   A. To do what they want.

   B. To help the computer to figure out problems for itself.

   C. To follow Martin Luther at all times.

   D. To type a password into the dashboard.

8. According to the passage, which function could be achieved on the basis of machine learning?

   A. Collecting information.   B. Voice recognition systems.

   C. Recording your location.   D. Video chat.

9. According to the passage, which of the following is **NOT** the dark side of big data?

   A. The police could send the patrols according to the records.

   B. We may be punished for invasion of privacy.

   C. Big data is going to steal our jobs.

   D. Big data is going to challenge white collars.

10. What is the challenge in the big data age?

    A. To protect our primacy.

    B. To protect our jobs.

    C. To safeguard free will, moral choice and other human rights.

    D. To safeguard the security of the world.

Text B The Big-data Revolution in Healthcare

⚙ Vocabulary

generate	['dʒenəret]	*vt.*	bring into existence 使形成；发生
streaming	['strimɪŋ]	*n.*	Streaming is a method of transmitting data from the Internet directly to a user's computer screen without the need to download it. 流媒体
tramp	[træmp]	*vi.*	If you tramp somewhere, you walk there slowly and with regular, heavy steps for a long time. 脚步沉重地

行走

| track | [træk] | *vt.* | If you track animals or people, you try to follow them by looking for the signs that they have left behind, for example, the marks left by their feet. 追踪 |
| prosecute | ['prɑsɪkjʊt] | *vt.* | charge somebody with a crime and put them on trial 对······提起诉讼 |

🅐 Activity One

*Direction: In this section, you will hear a talk **ONLY ONCE**. While listening, you may write **NO MORE THAN THREE WORDS** for each gap. Make sure the word(s) you fill in is (are) both grammatically and semantically acceptable. Now listen to the talk.*

The Big-data Revolution in Healthcare

A. There's a concept called "big data". What people are talking about is all of the information that we're generating through our **1.** _____ with and over the Internet.

B. For folks who work with big data, the biggest problem is: how do we **2.** _____ all that information?

C. But for people who are working in **3.** _____, the biggest problem is the data that would help them solve the problems is not actually **4.** _____ on the Internet. So we don't know, for example, how many people right now are being **5.** _____ disasters or by **6.** _____.

D. The reason why we don't know anything at all is that the **7.** _____ that we use in global health to find the data to solve these problems is terrible.

E. The only way we can actually find out how many children were **8.** _____ in the country of Indonesia, what **9.** _____ were vaccinated, is actually not on the **10.** _____, but by going out and knocking on doors.

🅑 Activity Two

Direction: Listen again and decide whether the following statements are true (T) or false (F).

11. The quality of the data typed into computer by the speaker is high without any mistake discovered. (   )

12. The Magpi is a software which allows people to create forms online. (   )

13. When you get the forms, you have to open them with a smart phone. (   )

14. The software is just like Hotmail. It's cloud based, and it doesn't require any training, programming, consultants. (   )

15. About 1,000 people find the website and use it in the second three years after we have the software. (   )

Post-Listening

Direction: Work in pairs and discuss the following questions.

1. What is the role of big data in the economic development?

2. What is the dark side of big data?

Section B Speaking

Analyzing or Explaining a Process

A process is a series of actions or events leading to an expected or planned outcome. There are two types of process speeches: those that instruct or direct (as discussed in Unit 5) and those that explain or analyze. Directional process speeches show the audience how to do something by steps, whereas an informational process speech explains or analyzes a process—it tells how something works or how something happened. For example, you could explain how World War II began or how hurricanes form as the result of a series of activities or events.

The purpose of an informational process speech is to inform, explain, or analyze. The audience should be gaining an understanding of the process, but he or she does not necessarily expect to be able to recreate the process. So an informational process speech is knowledge-intensive in its content, rational and logical in its organization. When you plan this kind of speech, you should bear in mind the following advice:

Be aware of the audience's knowledge level. Knowing how much your audience already know is important in deciding what to include and what to omit in the speech. For instance, suppose that you are explaining how the 2008 financial crisis happened to a group of bankers and investors, you should assume that the audience knows quite a lot about the process, so you should only include the latest or the most special findings. But if you are explaining the same thing to a group of high school students, you would have to approach the task differently. You would probably explain some basic concepts so that your audience may not be aware of.

Order the series of events logically. Since a process speech describes a sequence of actions or events leading to some preconceived end, it is reasonable that the actions and event be discussed in the order that they occur, or in other words, in chronological order. Other types of organization that may work for the explanation or analysis of a process include: order of importance, order of cause and effect, and order of category. You should decide on the order according to the nature of your topic. You may also prepare some handouts or PPT display to help your audience understand the sequence of events in the process.

Organize the speech in a plain, easy-to-follow way. To begin with, you should introduce the topic and establish the purpose for the speech so that the audience understands why the process is being described and analyzed. The actual process usually can be made up of three or four major actions or events in case the audience be confused by too many actions or events.

Questions to Think About

1. If you are to give a speech of process analysis in class and your classmates are to be your audience, what would you consider to be an appropriate topic? Your topic should be informative and understandable at the same time.

2. How are you going to get all the information you need for the topic you decide on in the previous question? If it is a topic that you are not very familiar with, what extra preparation do you need to make before you give the speech?

3. Using examples is an effective way to help your audience understand your analysis. What examples can you use for the topic you have chosen?

Communication Tasks

1. Choose one of the three topics and deliver a speech containing the process.

   (1) How does a pair of VR glasses work?

   (2) How are drugs addictive?

(3) Why does the U.K. intend to leave the E.U.?

2. What is a butterfly effect? Conduct a case study of a butterfly effect and get familiar with chain of events in its process. Then give a speech explaining this butterfly effect to your classmates.

Section C Exam Spotlight

① Activity One

*Direction: In this section, you will hear six short conversations. At the end of each conversation, a question will be asked about what was said. Both the conversations and the questions will be spoken **ONLY ONCE**. After each question there will be a pause. During the pause, you must read the four choices marked A, B, C, and D, and decide which one is the best answer.*

1. **A.** Ask Dr. Smith to alter his decision.   **B.** Ask Dr. Smith to call the library.

    C. Get the book directly from Dr. Smith.   **D.** Get Dr. Smith's written permission.

2. **A.** Disconnect his telephone.

    B. Blow a whistle into the receiver.

    C. Keep a record of incoming annoyance calls.

    D. Report his problem to the police.

3. **A.** He should move to another place.

    B. The neighbors probably won't turn down the music.

    C. He wants to listen to different music.

    D. He doesn't think the music is particularly loud.

4. **A.** Indifferent.   **B.** Worried.   **C.** Happy.   **D.** Indignant.

5. **A.** At a supermarket.   **B.** At a bar.

    C. At a library.   **D.** At a dormitory.

6. **A.** A driving test.   **B.** A traffic accident.

C. A police movie.   D. The best way to make signals.

② Activity Two

Direction: In this section, you will hear a passage. After listening, you should decide whether the following statements are true (T) or false (F).

7. One day the speaker's roommate heard him say he was on his way to the library for a certain book. (   )

8. She went to the library very quickly before the young man arrived. (   )

9. The speaker's roommate believed that the young man would not read the letter. (   )

10. The next day the young man came to the dormitory to return the letter. (   )

11. The book he borrowed was *Great Expectations*. (   )

③ Activity Three

Direction: Listen again and fill in the blanks in the following sentences based on the passage.

12. My roommate was interested in a young man in her English literature class, but she was _____ to let him know.

13. One day she overheard him say he was on his way to the library for a _____ book.

14. She _____ to the library, found the book and stuck in it a letter from her mother.

15. "He wouldn't, but if he's any kind of _____, he'll return it to me."

16. The next day he appeared with the letter and asked my roommate out on a _____.

④ Activity Four

Direction: In this section, you will hear a trainer giving a talk to people who want to learn outdoor survival skills. After listening, you will be given 20 seconds to complete the flow chart. Choose the best answer from the box to complete each blank. You will be given 20 seconds to fill in the blanks.

| **A.** air | **B.** ash | **C.** earth | **D.** grass | **E.** sticks | **F.** stones | **G.** water |

Making a Steam Pit

| Dig a pit |

↓

| Arrange a row of **17.** _____ over the pit |

↓

| Place **18.** _____ on top |

↓

| Light the wood and let it burn out |

↓

| Remove **19.** _____ |

↓

| Insert a stick |

↓

| Cover the pit with **20.** _____ |

↓

| Place wrapped food on top, and cover it with **21.** _____ |

↓

| Remove the stick and put **22.** _____ into the hole |

⑤ Activity Five

*Direction: Listen and choose **TWO** answers for each question.*

23. Which two characteristics apply to the bamboo oven?

   A. It's suitable for windy weather.

   B. The fire is lit below the bottom end of the bamboo.

   C. The bamboo is cut into equal lengths.

   D. The oven hangs from a stick.

   E. It cooks food by steaming it.

24. Which two pieces of advice does the speaker give about eating wild fungi?

   A. Cooking doesn't make poisonous fungi edible.

   B. Edible wild fungi can be eaten without cooking.

   C. Wild fungi are highly nutritious.

   D. Some edible fungi look very similar to poisonous varieties.

   E. Fungi which cannot be identified should only be eaten in small quantities.

⑥ Activity Six

*Direction: In this section, you will hear a passage **ONLY ONCE**. While listening, you may write **NO MORE THAN THREE WORDS** for each gap. Make sure the word(s) you fill in is (are) both grammatically and semantically acceptable. Now listen to the passage.*

Washington University is a **25.** _____ university. It has **26.** _____ students; 12% of them are international students, mostly **27.** _____ . The new school year that begins this fall will cost about $ 50,000 for undergraduates; that includes 12 months of living expenses **28.** _____ $20,000. Graduate tuition differs by program. The Master of **29.** _____ will cost about $38,000. The university offers **30.** _____ to international students. The university also offers a **31.** _____ to spread out the cost of tuition. It offers **32.** _____ .

Unit 11
Data Theft

Learning Objectives

- To know some major events concerning data leakage
- To learn how to protect your personal information from being disclosed
- To learn to guess the answer according to the key words while listening
- To learn to tell a story

Section A Listening

Pre-Listening

Direction: Work in pairs and discuss the following questions.

1. What will you do if your information were let out, such as date of birth, ID number, and telephone number?

2. Do you think any individual or organization that leaks personal privacy unintentionally should assume the legal liability?

Warm-up Activities

⚙ Vocabulary

law enforcement		*n.*	the job of making sure that the law is obeyed 法律的实施
punt	[pʌnt]	*n.*	kicking (a football) after it has dropped from the hands and before it touches the ground 悬空踢球
supervision	[ˌsʊpəˈvɪʒən]	*n.*	management by overseeing the performance or operation of a person or group 监督；管理
halt	[hɔlt]	*vt.*	(cause somebody or something) to stop temporarily （使某人 / 某事物）暂停

① Activity One

Direction: In this section, you will hear a news report. After listening, you should choose the best answer to each question. Now listen to the news report.

1. When did Yahoo acknowledge the data leakage of its users?

    A. On Thursday in early 2014.　　　　**B.** On Tuesday in early 2015.

    C. On Thursday in late 2014.　　　　**D.** On Tuesday in late 2015.

2. According to the news report, which of the following information is **NOT** stolen?

   A. Email address.   **B.** Hashed passwords.

   C. Bank account.   **D.** Date of birth.

3. Who did Yahoo plan to sell its core Internet business to?

   A. E-commerce giant Alibaba.   **B.** Verizon.

   C. Baidu.   **D.** None of the above.

② Activity Two

Direction: Listen to another news report and choose the best answer to each question.

4. What information do identity thieves steal?

   A. Telephone numbers.

   B. Social security numbers.

   C. Banking records.

   D. All of the above.

5. Which one is **NOT** the consequence for the victims?

   A. Reestablishment of financial history for years.

   B. Incapability of buying a house in the future.

   C. Being arrested for crimes in which they were not involved.

   D. Failure to find a job.

6. How do identity thieves get the information they need?

   A. By contriving a robbery.

   B. By seducing people into giving information on the telephone.

   C. By stealing documents containing personal information.

   D. Both B and C.

While-Listening

Text A Lessons from Data Theft of Yahoo

Vocabulary

desensitize	[ˌdi'sɛnsətaɪz]	*vt.*	make someone react less strongly to something by making them become used to it 使不敏感；使麻木不仁
infraction	[ɪn'frækʃən]	*n.*	an act of breaking a rule or law 违反；违背；破坏（法律）
unnerving	[ˌʌn'nɝvɪŋ]	*adj.*	making people feel worried or uncomfortable 使人紧张不安的
belie	[bɪ'laɪ]	*vt.*	give someone a false idea about something 掩饰
looting	[lutɪŋ]	*n.*	stealing things, especially from shops or homes that have been damaged in a war or riot 抢劫；洗劫；掠夺
encryption	[ɛn'krɪpʃən]	*n.*	the activity of converting from plain text into code 加密；数据加密
in jeopardy			in danger of harm, loss or destruction 处于危险境地
repercussion	[ˌripɚ'kʌʃən]	*n.*	indirect effect or result (especially unpleasant) of an event, etc.; consequence 令人不满意的后果；间接的影响（尤指不良的）

1 Activity One

Direction: In this section, you will hear a passage. After listening, you should choose the best answer to each question. Now listen to the passage.

1. Which of the following is **NOT** the question raised by the sheer scale of infraction?

A. Customers' worry about the company's management.

B. Public disclosure and issues over the future.

C. People's desperation about the data security on the Internet.

D. Whether Yahoo took enough care of its customers' personal data.

2. What makes the Yahoo case striking and unnerving?

A. It is the first case that discloses a large number of users' information.

B. It went apparently undetected for two years.

C. Yahoo shirks its responsibility after data leakage.

D. Not mentioned.

3. How much does Yahoo charge about its sale to Verizon?

A. $50 million.   B. $5 billion.

C. $4.8 billion.   D. $48 million.

4. What do the outdated and vulnerable encryption systems suggest?

A. The insufficient fund of Yahoo.   B. An uncomfortably lax security culture.

C. A lack of technical personnel.   D. The low credibility of Yahoo.

5. Why did consumers worry that the data breach may lead to their accounts at other sites being compromised?

A. Because the attackers are excellent in stealing information.

B. Because their passwords of other accounts were also stolen in this data breach.

C. Because many consumers use the same passwords on multiple platforms.

D. Because they forgot the passwords of their accounts at other sites.

❷ Activity Two

Direction: Listen again and decide whether the following statements are true (T) or false (F).

6. Although no high-value information were extracted, Yahoo should not shirk its responsibility for its failure to notice the cyber incursion. (   )

7. Yahoo adopted positive measures immediately in the wake of the discovery of the leakage, which is satisfactory for customers. (   )

8. Yahoo became aware of the scale of the problem at once when a breaching was being investigated. (   )

9. The deal between Yahoo and Verizon will be affected by the disclosures about Yahoo case. (   )

10. The massive stolen data was sold for $180 on the so-called dark web and was reported by *Vice Motherboard*. (　　)

Text B XcodeGhost—A Pretty Big Deal for Apple

⚙ Vocabulary

malicious	[mə'lɪʃəs]	*adj.*	very unkind and cruel, and deliberately behaving in a way that is likely to upset or hurt someone 怀有恶意的；恶毒的
stringent	['strɪndʒənt]	*adj.*	demanding strict attention to rules and procedures 严格的；严厉的
legitimate	[lə'dʒɪtəmɪt]	*adj.*	in accordance with the law or rules; lawful 公正的，正当的；合法的
malware	['mælwɛr]	*n.*	a computer program designed specifically to damage or disrupt a system, such as a virus 恶意软件（如病毒）

① Activity One

Direction: In this section, you will hear a passage. After listening, you should choose the best answer to each question. Now listen to the passage.

1. How many malicious software programs have been found in the App Store up to now?

　　A. Four.　　　　　　　　　　　　**B.** Five.

　　C. Six.　　　　　　　　　　　　　**D.** Seven.

2. How did the hackers embed the malicious software in these Apple apps?

　　A. By threatening the founder of legitimate programs to work for them.

　　B. By convincing developers to utilize counterfeit version of iOS and Mac apps.

　　C. By persuading developers to use pirated version of Apple's software.

　　D. By bribing the senior officials of cyber security firms.

3. According to Apple's spokeswoman, what did Apple do to cope with hacker attack?

　　A. Removing the apps created with counterfeit software from the App Store.

　　B. Working with developers to rebuild apps by using the proper version of Xcode.

C. Cooperating with police to arrest these hackers.

D. Both A and B.

4. Why is the malware attack regarded as "a pretty big deal"?

A. Because the App Store couldn't find a way out of the dilemma.

B. Because it could be hard to defend against if other attackers copy that approach.

C. Because the hackers would do anything evil to threaten our society.

D. Not mentioned.

5. According to the researchers, which one does **NOT** belong to the infected apps?

A. Didi Kuaidi.   B. A music app from NetEase.

C. Chat app WeChat.   D. A video app from Tencent.

Activity Two

Direction: Listen again and decide whether the following statements are true (T) or false (F).

6. XcodeGhost is a malicious program which was embedded in all the legitimate apps of cyber security firms. (   )

7. There had been such reports about malicious softwares making their way past Apple's approval process before this attack. (   )

8. iPhone and iPad users could take some steps to check whether their devices were infected. (   )

9. There have not been data theft or other harms in Palo Alto Networks up to now. (   )

10. Apple hasn't estimated how many apps had been tainted with XcodeGhost. (   )

Post-Listening

Direction: Work in pairs and discuss the following questions.

1. What do you think of data theft?

2. What can we do to prevent data theft?

Section **B** Speaking

Telling a Story

Are you a good story-teller or a story killer? Story-telling is a wonderful skill that can live up your communication and help you make friends. Anecdotes, parables, fables, allusions, metaphors and idioms are all story-telling methods for imparting wisdom or making a point. Frequently, such methods prove to be a far more effective way to achieve the speaker's purpose than through a plain presentation of facts and reasons. Yet, telling a story that can truly engage your audience is quite a challenge to most people. To begin with, you need to know the characteristics of a good story.

A good story is one with a point that the audience can relate to and will learn from. A good story has all or some of the following characteristics:

- The story fits the occasion.

- The story and its point address the issues at hand.

- The story is fresh and informative to the audience.

- The plot involves a transformation or a twist.

- The characters in the story come alive.

- The audience can relate to the story in some way and learn a lesson from it.

- The story-teller is sincere.

- The story is told well in a proper manner with a good taste.

When you see the need of telling a story and start preparing for it, you need to make clear the occasion and know the audience. Find out the purpose or the theme of the event, and get to know about the participants' interests and concerns. Both the point and the content of your story should fit in the occasion, respond to the audience's needs and serve their best interests. An old story that's been around for ten years is not likely to raise an eyebrow of the listeners. If the story successfully involve the audience and let them feel they are experiencing the story together with you, the audience will respond actively and favorably to it.

Regardless of the plot of the story, it should be told with sincerity and dignity. Exaggerated acts and mannerism should be used with caution unless you are a trained actor or actress. You may try to act out the characters in the story by mimicking their tone, accent or facial expression, but overdoing this may cause feeling of discomfort and distrust among your audience. You need to practice and try it out before your friends to make sure it will work for the occasion.

You also need to keep good timing. Try to finish the story and highlight its point within 3 to 5 minutes. Omit unimportant or irrelevant details, so you won't get tangled up in a complex, unfocused narration. If you finish the story by offering the audience a lesson and giving them something to think about, the audience will remember what you have told them and want more of your story next time.

In conclusion, remember that a good story contains many crucial elements. As a result, it is important to sit down and create stories that have some or all of the qualities discussed above.

Questions to Think About

1. What is a story twist? Use an example to illustrate this concept.

2. At a seminar about data safety and data theft, what kind of stories would fit the occasion and benefit the audience? Search the Internet for a good story that you can tell at this seminar.

3. Read some news and reports about data theft. What changes do you need to make to turn the news/reports into good stories?

Communication Tasks

1. Revise a report on data theft and create a story based on it. Then tell the story to your classmates. Your story should not be longer than 4 minutes.

2. Discuss with your classmates what you have learned about data safety from the stories you tell. Report the results of your discussion to your class.

3. Discuss what you have learned about story telling from your story-telling experience with your classmates. Report the results of your discussion to your class.

Section C Exam Spotlight

Activity One

Direction: In this section, you will hear a conversation. After listening, you should choose the best answer to each question. Now listen to the conversation.

1. **A.** Play snooker.　　　　　　　　**B.** Watch a film at the theater.

    C. Watch a video at the theater.　　**D.** Eat dinner.

2. **A.** He likes to sit there.　　　　　　**B.** The seats are nicer.

    C. The ticket price is lower.　　　　**D.** There is no ticket left for the front row.

② Activity Two

Direction: Listen again and fill in the blanks with the information you hear.

Evan's Address: **3.** _____

Evan's Phone Number: **4.** _____

Evan's Postcode: **5.** _____

Susan ordered a **6.** _____ and a **7.** _____ .

Susan gave **8.** _____ to Evan.

The discount for senior students is **9.** _____ .

Evan had mashed potatoes and a **10.** _____ .

③ Activity Three

Direction: In this section, you will hear a conversation among two students and their tutor about the presentation they are going to make at the tutorial class. After listening, you should choose the best answer to each question.

11. **A.** A little boring.

    B. Very attractive.

    C. They took too many notes.

12. **A.** He was uneasy when making it.

    B. He is not satisfied with it.

    C. It is strongly argued.

13. **A.** 83%.　　　　　　**B.** 87%.　　　　　　**C.** 78%.

14. **A.** He reads slowly.

    B. He lacks vocabulary.

C. He cannot understand the complex reading materials.

15. **A.** To choose an easiest part.

    B. To help the intensive reading.

    C. To get the main idea of the passage.

16. **A.** After a lot of reading.

    B. After writing some essays.

    C. After doing basic programs.

④ Activity Four

*Direction: In this section, you will hear a passage **THREE TIMES**. When the passage is read for the first time, you should listen carefully for its general idea. When the passage is read for the second time, you are required to fill in the blanks either with the exact words you have just heard or the main points in your own words. Finally, when the passage is read for the third time, you should check what you have written.*

The tourist industry differs from many others in that it employs more women than many other kinds of business. Indeed, women are **17.** _____ at all levels—from the semi-skilled to management positions—in the transportation companies. Many **18.** _____ travel agents are women who have **19.** _____ independent enterprises after gaining **20.** _____ elsewhere in the industry.

Experience is necessary for the successful **21.** _____ of a travel agency. It has been **22.** _____ that a minimum of ten years' work in the industry is a prerequisite for setting up an agency with the **23.** _____ of making it a success. There are many different ways to acquire the necessary experience. Some agents begin as clerical workers or **24.** _____ in travel agencies or in the transportation companies. **25.** _____

_____. In addition to dealing with the public, the travel agent must deal with people who work for the other components in the industry. **26.** _____

_____. Even when help is available, as it usually is from the airlines, the agent who can compute fares accurately has an advantage over one who cannot. **27.** _____

_____.

⑤ Activity Five

*Direction: In this section, you will hear a short passage **ONLY ONCE**. While listening, you may write **NO MORE THAN THREE WORDS** for each gap. Now listen to the passage.*

If you are a graduate student, you may **28.** _____ your adviser for many things, including help with improving grades, acquiring **29.** _____, forming an **30.** _____ and getting letters of recommendation. If you are a **31.** _____, your adviser also may be your "boss".

Academic departments vary in their procedures for assigning academic advisers to graduate students. In some departments, either the **32.** _____ or the director of graduate studies serves for at least the first semester as a new student adviser. Then students select an adviser, based on **33.** _____. In other departments, a new student is assigned a faculty adviser based on some system of distribution of the department's "advising load". Later, students may have the opportunity of selecting the adviser that they prefer.

In any case, new graduate students can learn who their advisers or **34.** _____ advisers are by visiting or emailing the departmental office and asking for the information. Graduation requirements **35.** _____ the number of credits you must earn, the minimum grade point average you must achieve and the distribution of credits you must have from among differing departments or fields of study.

In addition, it is necessary to apply for graduation when you are near the time that you will be completing your graduation requirements. Since graduation requirements vary among **36.** _____ of the university, you should **37.** _____ the Bulletin of Information. You should also direct your questions to your departmental office or academic adviser.

Unit 12
Self-driving Car

Learning Objectives

- To learn to find out implied information
- To learn to talk about your own opinions about novel technology
- To learn more skills of presenting a product

<h1 style="text-align:center">Section Ⓐ Listening</h1>

Pre-Listening

Direction: Work in pairs and discuss the following questions.

1. Have you heard of self-driving technology? What is it?

2. What do you think of self-driving technology?

Warm-up Activities

⚙ Vocabulary

steering	[stɪrɪŋ]	*n.*	equipment or mechanism for turning the direction of a car, boat, etc. 转向装置；操舵装置
pedal	[ˈpɛdl]	*n.*	a part in a car or on a machine that you press with your foot to control it 踏板
bolster	[ˈbolstɚ]	*vt.*	give support to somebody/something; strengthen or reinforce 支持；加强（某事物）
minivan	[ˈmɪnɪvæn]	*n.*	(AmE) a large car with seats for six to eight people （美语）商务车

① Activity One

Direction: In this section, you will hear a news report. After listening, you should choose the best answer to each question. Now listen to the news report.

1. What will you **NOT** see in Ford's new driverless car?

    A. A car seats.   **B.** Wheels.

    C. A steering wheel.   **D.** Lights.

2. Which Chinese search engine has Ford cooperated with?

   A. Sogou.   **B.** Baidu.

   C. Sina.   **D.** Tencent.

3. How much has Ford invested in laser-based driverless system company Velodyne Lidar?

   A. $75 million.   **B.** $175 million.

   C. $750 million.   **D.** $50 million.

➋ Activity Two

Direction: Listen to another news report and choose the best answer to each question.

4. What is Gett?

   A. It is a car brand.

   B. It is a company that develops self-driving technology.

   C. It is a taxi-booking service system.

   D. It is a search engine's name.

5. How much has General Motors invested in Lyft?

   A. $500 million.   **B.** $150 million.

   C. $50 million.   **D.** $550 million.

6. Why had Ford decided to leap to full autonomy?

   A. Because it is the safer way.

   B. Because it is more efficient.

   C. Because it can be easier to control.

   D. Because they had not found a technology that could ensure driver engagement when not in control.

While-Listening

Text A — U.S. Government's First Formal Guideline for Self-driving Cars

⚙ Vocabulary

hamper	['hæmpə]	*vt.*	make it difficult for someone to do something 妨碍；阻碍
patchwork	['pætʃwɜːk]	*n.*	thing made of various small pieces or parts 拼凑的东西
autonomous	[ɔ'tɑnəməs]	*adj.*	self-governing; acting independently 自治的；自主的；自发的

① Activity One

Direction: In this section, you will hear a news report. After listening, you should choose the best answer to each question. Now listen to the news report.

1. Which one can **NOT** be used to describe the autonomous vehicles according to the passage?

   A. It can make transportation more expensive.

   B. It can make transportation safer.

   C. It can make transportation cleaner.

   D. It can make transportation more efficient.

2. What do the new rules focus on?

   A. Price.   B. Safety.

   C. Technology issues.   D. Car-making process.

3. How many points does the assessment for car makers have in total?

   A. 5.   B. 50.   C. 15.   D. 55.

4. According to the rule of California, which kind of cars will be banned from public roads for at least three years?

   A. Cars without a steering wheel.   B. Cars without a pedal.

   C. Cars without a wheel.   D. Cars without car lights.

5. What is the goal of the guidelines from the Department of Transportation?

   A. To make a regulatory framework for the car makers.

   B. To make a regulatory framework for the public road.

   C. To create a more safer transportation system.

   D. To create a consistent national regulatory framework.

② Activity Two

Direction: Listen again and decide whether the following statements are true (T) or false (F).

6. There are a few formal guidelines for self-driving cars before. (   )

7. President Barack Obama has made his support for driverless vehicles a key part of his tech agenda. (   )

8. Google is developing self-driving cars without a steering wheel. (   )

9. Individual states must all follow the guidelines from the Department of Transportation over the autonomous vehicles. (   )

10. The National Highway Traffic Safety Administration will gain new authority to regulate self-driving cars, including the ability to issue recalls if it deems cars are unsafe. (   )

Text B Google's New Self-driving Car

⚙ Vocabulary

prototype	['protə'taɪp]	*n.*	the first form that a new design of a car, machine, etc. has, or a model of it used to test the design before it is produced（新型汽车、机器等的）原型；雏形

① Activity One

*Direction: In this section, you will hear a passage **ONLY ONCE**. While listening, you may write **NO MORE THAN THREE WORDS** for each gap. Make sure the word(s) you fill in is (are) both grammatically and semantically acceptable. Now listen to the passage.*

Google's New Self-driving Car

I. Eliminating human error

Sergey Brin is a co-founder of Google. He says the computer-controlled cars can eliminate, or end, driving mistakes **1.** _____ humans. Experts say **2.** _____ of the 1.2 million yearly road deaths are caused by human error. Self-driving cars could also improve areas of high traffic and especially help older people and **3.** _____ people.

Google first announced that it was working on a driverless car **4.** _____. Mr. Brin says Google does not want to be a car company, but wants automakers to use its technology.

Critics worry about the safety of having cars without **5.** _____. And, Google admits there have been minor accidents in the six years it has been testing autonomous cars.

II. Can it be trusted?

Critics also question the dependability of self-driving cars. They wonder if the cars can be trusted to work **6.** _____. They also ask if such cars **7.** _____ people.

In 2013, J.D. Power and Associates did a study of U.S. drivers. It found that only **8.** _____ was interested in a fully autonomous car.

Mr. Urmson says Google needs to do a better job of educating people about self-driving technology. He also says Google needs to better inform the public about its **9.** _____ with the technology.

The company is building a website to do that. The site will include a monthly report that will include details of any accidents involving Google cars. It will also permit people to **10.** _____ any experiences they might have with the cars.

② Activity Two

Direction: Listen again and decide whether the following statements are true (T) or false (F).

11. The two-seat vehicle does not need a gas pedal or steering wheel. (   )

12. The new vehicle is designed for long trips. (   )

13. The vehicle is electric and has to be recharged after 130 kilometers. (   )

14. Google is worried about the record of the autonomous car test. (   )

Direction: *Work in pairs and discuss the following questions.*

1. What do you think of self-driving cars?

2. What regulation would you like to propose about self-driving cars if you were a government official?

Presenting a Product (1)

Many companies use presentation software such as PowerPoint slide shows as part of a new product launch strategy. The PowerPoint software allows you to combine text, graphics and/or video to communicate the new product story while making the message interesting enough to attract and impress audience. Usually in a formal product presentation, the maximum number of slides is twenty, at two minutes a slide. If you provide your customers with too much information, you may confuse them.

In a product presentation, there are the following eight parts you can include:

Introduction: This is normally the part where the speaker introduces him/herself, and the point of the product presentation. This is where you want to hook your audience and tell them what is in it for them.

Agenda: This part is optional. It tells your audience what you are going to cover in your presentation.

Company information: This is a way to establish credibility of your company with the audience. You don't need to spend a lot of time on this, but you need to hold the audience's attention with compelling information about your company.

Positioning: Successful products have a unique technology or positioning that sets them apart from other products on the market. You want to introduce this aspect of your product to let your audience know how your product is different and why they should listen to the rest of your presentation. Talk about the uniqueness of your product in terms of the audience's problem or pain—they have a problem and your product is solving this problem. This part of your presentation must be very precise, crisp and to the point.

Product description: You should clearly describe your product in terms that your audience will understand. It may be helpful to have a chart with the product components. You want to give the audience a frame of reference for the features and benefits that they are going to see. You also want them to know how your product fits into their existing environment.

Benefits: You need to clearly specify the benefits of your product to your target audience. You can make a list of all the features and benefits embodied by your product. They may be obvious to you because you know the product well, but your audience should have them clearly called out and they must relate to their needs.

Examples/Successes: At this point in the presentation your audience should be familiar with your product and why it is different and better. In order to drive this point home, use examples of how your product is being used and how customers have benefited from the product.

Closure: This is your opportunity for a "call to action". You may summarize and reiterate the point of the presentation and include product pricing in this section. Finally you can ask your audience to do something, like trying a sample or placing an order.

It is important to note that not all of the eight points are necessarily included in any product presentations. Some of them might be omitted, but you must include positioning, product description and benefits.

Questions to Think About

1. When you prepare your PPT slides, what type of slide layout and design should you choose and why?

2. What would be the advantages and disadvantages of using a cartoon-style template for your PPT?

3. What graphics or pictures can you include in your product presentation?

4. Think about the phone, the computer or other products you are using. What is the positioning of these products? Or in other words, what makes them unique and beneficial to you?

Communication Tasks

1. Steve Jobs has been loved and admired by his fans for the engaging presentations he has made about Apple products. What do you think are the major strengths of his presentations? Discuss with your classmates and exchange your ideas.

2. A Google self-driving car is an autonomous car developed by Google X as part of its project to develop technology for mainly electric cars. Do some research and find out the positioning and benefits of the Google self-driving car in groups.

3. A driverless car, also called an autonomous car or robotic car, makes use of a variety of techniques such as radar, GPS, computer vision, artificial intelligence, etc. to detect surroundings and identify appropriate navigation paths. Explore one key technology used in driverless cars and introduce that technology to your classmates.

Section C Exam Spotlight

1 Activity One

Direction: In this section, you will hear some announcements from railway stations and airports. These announcements give information to travelers about trains and planes. For each announcement that you hear, write in the box below the platform number, flight number, time and destination.

Trains

	Platform No.	Time	Destination
1.			
2.			
3.			
4.			

Planes

	Flight No.	Time	Destination
5.			
6.			
7.			
8.			

② Activity Two

Direction: In this section, you will hear a talk about a physics class. After listening, answer the following questions with **NO MORE THAN THREE WORDS** *for each answer.*

9. When was the talk probably given?

    _____

10. What does the speaker mainly talk about?

    _____

11. What can students do if they miss a test?

    _____

12. On which days does the professor have office hours?

    _____

③ Activity Three

Direction: In this section, you will hear a short lecture. After listening, you should choose the best answer to each question.

13. **A.** Listening.　　**B.** Speaking.　　**C.** Reading.　　**D.** Writing.

14. **A.** Lose 10 points.　**B.** Lose 15 points.　**C.** Not be accepted.　**D.** Not be graded.

15. **A.** Absence of class.　**B.** Four tests.　**C.** Quizzes.　**D.** Six theme papers.

16. **A.** Monday.　　**B.** Wednesday.　　**C.** Thursday.　　**D.** Friday.

④ Activity Four

Direction: In this section, you will hear a lecture about the history of chess. After listening, you should complete the summary below. Write **NO MORE THAN THREE WORDS** *for each answer.*

The History of Chess

Chess originated in either Afghanistan or **17.** _____ around the year 600 AD. However, the game might even be **18.** _____ years old.

There is international agreement on the **19.** _____, but some variations exist, e.g., in Japan and **20.** _____.

The version played in Europe and America came from Iran and was established in Italy and Spain around the year 1000 AD. The Vikings took it to Scandinavia and it had reached Central Europe by **21.** _____ AD and by then the rules we use today were in place.

The **22.** _____ used today in championships originated in the 19th century and were named after an English chess champion.

The first official championship took place in 1866 in London. To avoid running overtime, they used a **23.** _____.

The winner was from Bohemia—in effect the first **24.** _____.
He held the record until 1894 when he was beaten by a German-born American who was then beaten by a Cuban named Capablanca. Some people rank Capablanca among the **25.** _____ who ever lived.

Also in this league was Bobby Fischer—the first **26.** _____ to become World Chess Champion.

⑤ Activity Five

*Direction: In this section, you will hear a passage **ONLY ONCE**. After listening, you should fill in the blanks. Now listen to the passage.*

New words enter the English language all the time. In fact, English has always been in a state of **27.** _____. And in recent years, **28.** _____ words and phrases have entered the language. But where do all these new words come from? Words come out of the culture that they represent and they **29.** _____. So if you've got a new development in medicine, for example, bird flu, then you'll get a new word coming out of that. If there is a **30.** _____ conflict, that may well bring **31.** _____ of new words to the fore. Going back **32.** _____, the First and Second World Wars were times of great creativity of language because people from different countries met each other and exchanged their words and words developed from there. So, words come from the playground. They come from **33.** _____. They come from any area of life, because every area of life is changing from **34.** _____. And does English have more words than any other language? It certainly has more than other **35.** _____ and probably more than any other language in the world. English is put together from so many different bits. Originally, it was a Germanic language. And then after the Norman conquest in 1066, there was **36.** _____ influx of French words. And it comes from a country, the United Kingdom, which was quite an expansive trading colonial power in the past. And all these have brought all sorts of other new words into the language.

Unit 13
3D Printing

Learning Objectives

- To learn the development of 3D printing in the world
- To learn how 3D printers operate
- To learn expressions of high technology
- To learn to present a product

Section **A** Listening

Pre-Listening

Direction: Work in pairs and discuss the following questions.

1. What do you know about 3D printing?

2. What fields will 3D printing be applied into?

Warm-up Activities

⚙ Vocabulary

impaired	[ɪmˈpɛrd]	*adj.*	damaged, less strong, or not as good as before 受损的
Vienna	[vɪˈɛnə]	*n.*	the capital and largest city of Austria 维也纳（奥地利首都）
robe	[rob]	*n.*	a long loose piece of clothing, especially one worn for official ceremonies 长袍；礼服
entangled	[ɪnˈtæŋgld]	*adj.*	twisted together in a tangled mass 卷入的；被缠住的
bookmark	[ˈbʊkmark]	*n.*	a piece of paper, leather, etc. that put in a book to show you the last page you have read 书签

① Activity One

Direction: In this section, you will hear a short passage. After listening, you should choose the best answer to each question. Now listen to the passage.

1. According to the short passage, what is *The Kiss*?

   A. A museum in Vienna, Austria.

   B. A book written by Gustav Klimt.

   C. A painting printed with new technology.

   D. A 3D model designed by Dominika Raditsch.

2. Who is Dominika Raditsch?

    A. The manager of the Belvedere Museum.

    B. A technician who made 3D versions of artwork in 2010.

    C. A blind museum visitor.

    D. A famous painter in Austria.

3. According to the passage, where do the artworks have reproductions that can be touched?

    A. At the art exhibition in Europe.

    B. At the Prado in Madrid, Spain.

    C. At the Belvedere Museum in Vienna, Austria.

    D. Both B and C.

② Activity Two

Direction: Listen to another passage and choose the best answer to each question.

4. What's the difference between Facebook's new service and other smart phone applications?

    A. Users can order food with discount coupon and buy tickets on Facebook.

    B. Users can organize their friends' most favorite places and things in one place much easier on Facebook.

    C. Users can make appointments with strangers in Facebook.

    D. Users can work at home by way of using Facebook.

5. Which of the following statements is **INCORRECT**?

    A. Users can order food directly from Facebook pages of some restaurants on Facebook.

    B. Facebook expands its offerings by providing more new services, cutting down the time people spend on using social media apps.

    C. Users have the chance to officially endorse a political candidate on the Facebook.

    D. The company launched a feature called Marketplace, where people can buy and sell things locally.

6. Which of the following expressions is **TRUE**?

    A. The company has not started the use of Facebook at work, which would help people connect in the workplace.

    B. Users can order personnel services on Facebook, such as getting a haircut.

C. Facebook is testing its service around the world and will be offered to international users in the future.

D. Users cannot choose which Facebook friends can see their endorsements.

While-Listening

Text A 3D Printing in China

⚙ Vocabulary

hopper	['hɑpɚ]	*n.*	a large cone-shaped device into which substances such as grain, coal, or animal food can be put and from which they can be released when required 料斗；漏斗
foundry sand		*n.*	silica-based sand mixed with clay, oil, etc. to improve its cohesive strength, used in moulding 铸造用砂
behemoth	[bɪ'himɔθ]	*n.*	something that is very large 庞然大物
titanium	[taɪ'tenɪəm]	*n.*	a strong light silver-white metal that is used to make aircraft and spacecraft, and is often combined with other metals [化学] 钛（金属元素）
fuselage	['fjuzəlɑʒ]	*n.*	the main part of a plane, in which people sit or goods are carried（飞机的）机身
landing-gear		*n.*	an aircraft's wheels and other parts that support them 起落架；起落装置，着陆装置
tour de force		*n.*	something that is done very skillfully and successfully, and is very impressive 绝技；精心杰作
acrylonitrile	[ˌækrəlo'naɪtrəl]	*n.*	a colorless liquid unsaturated nitrile made from propene [有化] 丙烯腈；氰乙烯
butadiene	[ˌbjʊtə'daɪin]	*n.*	a colorless easily liquefiable flammable gas that polymerizes readily and is used mainly in the manufacture of synthetic rubbers [有化] 丁二烯
styrene	['staɪrin]	*n.*	a colorless oily volatile flammable water-insoluble liquid made from ethylene and benzene [有化] 苯乙烯

❶ Activity One

Direction: In this section, you will hear a passage. After listening, you should choose the best answer to each question. Now listen to the passage.

1. What kind of customers does AFS mainly serve?

    A. Foundry and vehicle repair plants.

    B. Aerospace firms and metal smelting factories.

    C. Automobile manufacturers and aerospace companies.

    D. None of the above.

2. How long does it take to make a prototype car engine for conventional machine shop?

    A. Two weeks.   **B.** Two months.

    C. Several months.   **D.** Not mentioned.

3. What is China's largest 3D printer used for?

    A. To save time and money when building planes.

    B. To build planes to replace Airbus and Boeing.

    C. To make large and complex parts for China's commercial aircraft programme.

    D. To make contributions to the National Laboratory for Aeronautics and Astronautics.

4. Which of the following differences between Tiertime's printers and those of AFS is **TRUE**?

    A. Tiertime's printers operate on factory floors, while those of AFS sit in designers' offices.

    B. AFS' printers cost up to 1.5 million yuan, while most of Tiertime's printers sell for less than 6,000 yuan.

    C. AFS' printers allow people to print their ideas directly, while those of Tiertime cannot print in this way.

    D. Tiertime's printers sit in designers' offices, while those of AFS operate on factory floors.

❷ Activity Two

Direction: Listen again and decide whether the following statements are true (T) or false (F).

5. William Zeng is a general manager assistant of AFS. (   )

6. Selling the laser-sintering printers it makes to others is one of the pillar industries of AFS.
    (   )

7. Making titanium fuselage frames and high-strength steel landing-gear from precast metal will be a technical tour de force. (　　)

8. Tiertime, as one of the biggest firms in the field of 3D printers, is situated in the suburbs of Beijing. (　　)

9. According to some officials, 3D printers will probably be introduced into schools to arouse students' interest in careers in engineering. (　　)

10. 3D printing can replace mass manufacturing soon. (　　)

Text B Print Me a Phone

⚙ Vocabulary

circuitry	['sɜ·kɪtrɪ]	n.	a system of electric circuits 电路；电路系统
lithography	[lɪ'θɑgrəfɪ]	n.	a method of planographic printing from a metal or stone surface 平版印刷术，石印术
inkjet	['ɪŋk'dʒet]	n.	a type of computer printing that recreates a digital image by propelling droplets of ink onto paper, plastic, or other substrates 喷墨；印刷
resistor	[rɪ'zɪstɚ]	n.	a piece of wire or other material used for increasing electrical resistance [电] 电阻器
versatile	['vɜ·sətl]	adj.	having many different uses 多用途的，多功能的
nanometer	['nænə͵mitɚ]	n.	a metric unit of length equal to one billionth of a meter [计量] 纳米；毫微米
minuscule	['mɪnəskjul]	adj.	extremely small 极小的
armour	['ɑmɚ]	n.	metal plates covering warships, tanks, etc. to protect them from shells, missles, etc. 装甲板
thermoplastic	[͵θɜ·mo'plæstɪk]	adj.	(plastic substance) that becomes soft and easy to bend when heated and hardens when cooled 热塑性的

❶ Activity One

Direction: In this section, you will hear a short passage. After listening, you should choose the best
answer to each question. Now listen to the passage.

1. Which of the following belongs to printing electronics?

   A. Screen printing.   **B.** Lithography.

   C. Inkjet.   **D.** All of the above.

2. According to the passage, what is Xerox?

   A. A research center in Canada.   **B.** A company in the U.S.

   C. A software system.   **D.** A silver ink.

3. According to the passage, at what temperature can a silver ink melt?

   A. 962 ℃.   **B.** 142 ℃.

   C. 121 ℃.   **D.** 200 ℃.

4. Which of the following is **NOT** the component whose circuits can be printed by a silver ink?

   A. Sensors.   **B.** Personal computers.

   C. Flexible display screens.   **D.** Antennae for radio-frequency security tags.

5. What is the most difficult part for Optomec to print a phone?

   A. Edge circuits for screen.   **B.** The chips.

   C. Multiple-layer circuits.   **D.** Touch-screen.

❷ Activity Two

Direction: Listen again and decide whether the following statements are true (T) or false (F).

6. The process of assembling circuit boards, components and bundles of wire into an electronic device is costly and labor intensive. (   )

7. By incorporating circuitry and components into raw material, printing electronics in three dimensions would greatly change the way electronic goods are made. (   )

8. During chemical-etching processes, only a small quantity of silver is used and there is no waste. (   )

9. Additive-manufacturing system can print a GPS on the case of a mobile phone for higher localization accuracy. (   )

10. Optomec is developing applications which can print antennae, battery, touch-screen parts and three-dimensional connections for chips. (   )

Post-Listening

Direction: Work in pairs and discuss the following questions.

1. What do you want to print if you have a 3D printer? Why?

2. Is there any disadvantage of 3D printer?

Section B Speaking

Presenting a Product (2)

Product demonstration is a promotional presentation often used when companies launch a new product for the first time. In many cases, this will be the customer's first introduction to the product. Product presentations are an important part of selling your product to prospective customers, for first impressions are critical.

Product presentations are not simply sales pitches. A product presentation should enable potential consumers to see the product, to know about its superior or unique features, and to have an understanding of how it works. It should convince the audience or prospective buyers of its value and advantage. Yet, a product presentation should never be a tour of a product's features and functions. Instead, it should involve the customer's experience with the product playing a key role. In other words, the presenter takes the audience on an experience of using and testing the product.

When you start planning your product presentation, be sure you know the following information:

Target audience information: Your audience will largely define the objective of your presentation. Before you demonstrate a product, do your research and find out: Who are you giving the presentation to, prospective customers, investors, or management? What are their needs and immediate concerns? Where is their pain? Gather some specific information about the people or group who'll be attending the presentation and make sure that your data and content are uniquely matched to the audience.

Industry information: This is key to wisely positioning your product in the industry and in the market. What is the industry like right now? Check information from the latest industry conference, press releases, annual reports, published interviews and so forth to fully understand the context of the industry and your competitors. Being an expert of your industry will add to your credibility and add to the effectiveness of your presentation.

Company information: If yours is a start-up or a relatively not so well known company, you need to let the audience have some knowledge about your company. This is a way to establish credibility and to make the audience feel comfortable with your company. You need to relate to the history and some important facts about your company so as to create a positive, promising impression. Interesting facts to know also include customer lists, high-profile executives or advisors, awards and major milestones.

Product information: A product presenter should know everything there is to know about the product he/she is presenting. Talk to designers, engineers, product managers and the salespeople to get a whole set of product data that can be used in your presentation, including technical specifications, special features, materials, price, distribution channels, etc.

Once you have all this information, you can start to create your own product presentation.

Questions to Think About

1. Why is it necessary to know about the industry the product belongs to?

2. When you are presenting the same product to investors and customers, would there be any differences in your presentation? What differences would there be?

3. What information and facts about a company can help to create a positive, promising impression of it?

4. Do you think a product presenter should fully understand the technical details of a product? Why or why not?

Communication Tasks

1. Select a small local company. Gather some information about this company and do a 1-minute company introduction. Try to create a positive and promising image of the company with your introduction.

2. Explore the Internet and find a company that offers personalized 3D printing services and products. Gather information about the company and create a company profile for it.

3. What is your dream smart phone like? What design and functions would you like your dream phone to have? Design your own dream phone and present your ideas of an ideal phone to your class.

4. The Ultimaker 2+ is considered to be one of the most solid, all-around 3D printers on the market in 2016. Gather information about this 3D printer and present the information to your classmates.

Section C Exam Spotlight

1 Activity One

Direction: *In this section, you will hear a conversation. For questions 1–7, you should fill in the blanks with* **NO MORE THAN TWO WORDS** *for each answer. For question 8, you should choose* **THREE** *answers.*

Booking Form	
Example	Answer
Agency's Name	Dream Time Travel
1. Full Name: _____	
2. Source of Information: _____ *Magazine*	
3. Destination: _____	
4. Number of People: _____	
5. Departure of Date: _____	
6. Length of Holiday: _____	
7. Type of Insurance: _____	

8. Which **THREE** options does the woman want to book? _____

A. Breakfast.	**B.** Night safari.
C. Tennis.	**D.** Room with a balcony.
E. Beauty therapy.	**F.** Trip to beach.
G. Dinner.	

② Activity Two

Direction: In this section, you will hear an introduction to the college library services. For questions 9–11, you should choose the best answer to each question. For questions 12–14, you should decide whether the statements are true (T) or false (F).

9. **A.** On the ground floor. **B.** On the first floor.
    C. On the second floor. **D.** On the third floor.

10. **A.** Novels. **B.** Indexed journals.
    C. Fiction. **D.** Course books.

11. **A.** Photocopy services. **B.** Microforms.
    C. Computer services. **D.** Typewriters.

12. Prospective students have the chance to use the library during vacations. (   )

13. The library is only for college students' use. (   )

14. The library doesn't open on weekends. (   )

③ Activity Three

Direction: Listen to a lecture on health and complete the table. Match the appropriate letters A–I with questions 15–21. You can choose more than one letter.

A. has beta-carotene.
B. are not fattening.
C. are primarily carbohydrates.
D. are most nutritious when they are eaten fresh and raw.
E. contains compounds that appear to protect against colon cancer.

F. contain vitamin C.

G. protect against heart disease and high blood pressure.

H. plays an important role in keeping your digestive tract healthy.

I. is a good high-fibre snack.

Items	Facts
15. Whole grains	
16. Vegetables	
17. Cantaloupe	
18. Oranges and orange juice	
19. Vegetables in the cabbage family	
20. Fibre	
21. Popcorn	

④ Activity Four

*Direction: In this section, you will hear a short passage **ONLY ONCE**. While listening, you may write **NO MORE THAN THREE WORDS** for each gap. Now listen to the passage.*

Limiting the Growth of Technology

Throughout history, man has changed his physical environment to improve his way of life. With the tools of technology, man has **22.** _____ many physical features of the Earth. He has **23.** _____ woodland into farmland. He has **24.** _____ the face of the Earth by cutting through mountains to build roads and railways. However, these changes in the physical environment have not always had **25.** _____. Today, pollution of the air and water is a danger to the health of the **26.** _____. Each day thousands of **27.** _____ come out of vehicles. Smoke from factories pollutes the air of **28.** _____ and the surrounding countryside. The air in cities is becoming increasingly unhealthy. The pollution of water is **29.** _____ harmful. In the sea, pollution from oil is killing a lot of **30.** _____ and fish. It is now necessary for man to limit the growth of technology in order to **31.** _____ on Earth.

Unit 14
Artificial Intelligence

Learning Objectives

- To learn basic knowledge of AI
- To learn to guess the meaning of listening materials
- To learn to express thanks

Section Ⓐ Listening

Pre-Listening

Direction: Work in pairs and discuss the following questions.

1. What is artificial intelligence? Have you ever used it?

2. Do you think artificial intelligence is prevalent in our daily life? Please give an example.

Warm-up Activities

⚙ Vocabulary

vaccine	[væk'sin]	*n.*	a substance containing a virus or bacterium in a form that is not harmful, given to a person or animal to prevent them from getting the disease that the virus or bacterium causes 疫苗
combination	[ˌkɑmbɪ'neʃən]	*n.*	the mixture you get when two or more things are combined 混合物
mapping	['mæpɪŋ]	*n.*	the activity or process of making a map 绘图
approximation	[əˌprɑksə'meʃən]	*n.*	a number, calculation, or position that is close to a correct number, time, or position, but is not exact 近似值
curb	[kɝb]	*n.*	stone or concrete edge of a pavement at the side of a road（镶石的）路缘，路边

① Activity One

Direction: In this section, you will hear a short passage. After listening, you should choose the best answer to each question. Now listen to the passage.

1. Which area is AI just entering into?

   A. Public health area.   **B.** Healthcare industry.

C. IT area.   **D.** West medicine area.

2. What is the negative influence when having more than 800 medicines and vaccines to treat cancer?

    A. There are less options to choose from.

    B. There are more than a thousand medicines to choose from.

    C. Too many options make it difficult to choose right drugs for patients.

    D. Too many options make it easy to choose drugs for patients.

3. What is the goal of the machine called "Hanover"?

    A. It aims to help doctors choose the most effective drugs for patients.

    B. It aims to memorize all the papers.

    C. It aims to help predict wrong drug.

    D. It helps to remember those papers necessary to cancer.

② Activity Two

Direction: Listen to another passage and choose the best answer to each question.

4. How many companies are there applying AI into the creation of driverless cars and in which year?

    A. Over 13, 2016.   **B.** Over 30, 2016.

    C. Over 13, 1916.   **D.** Over 30, 1960.

5. Which of the following is **NOT** mentioned when talking about those incorporated systems?

    A. Braking.   **B.** Collision prevention.

    C. Lane keeping.   **D.** Mapping.

6. What is the major factor that influences the ability for a driverless car to function?

    A. Lane changing.

    B. Mapping.

    C. Data on the approximation of street light.

    D. Pre-programming.

While-Listening

Text A Existential Risk from Advanced Artificial Intelligence

⚙ Vocabulary

existential	[ˌɛgzɪˈstɛnʃəl]	*adj.*	relating to or dealing with existence 存在主义的；存在的
celebrity	[səˈlɛbrətɪ]	*n.*	someone who is famous 名人
titan	[taɪtn]	*n.*	a person who is very important, powerful, strong, big, clever, etc. 巨人；巨头
convergent	[kənˈvɝdʒənt]	*adj.*	coming closer together 会聚性的；集中的
humanity	[hjʊˈmænətɪ]	*n.*	people in general; being humane 人类
ultimately	[ˈʌltɪmətlɪ]	*adv.*	finally; after a series of things have happened 最后；最终
hypothetical	[ˌhaɪpəˈθɛtɪkəl]	*adj.*	imagined or suggested but not necessarily real or true 假设的；假定的
counterargument	[ˈkaʊntəˌɑrgjʊmənt]	*n.*	an argument against another argument, idea, or suggestion 抗辩；辩论
intrinsically	[ɪnˈtrɪnsɪkəlɪ]	*adv.*	being part of the nature or character of someone or something 本质上地
high-profile	[haɪˈprofaɪl]	*adj.*	attracting a lot of attention and interest from the public and newspapers, television, etc. 备受瞩目的
militarized	[ˈmɪlətəˈraɪzd]	*adj.*	A militarized area, country, or organization has a large, strong army and other armed forces and many weapons. 军事化的

❶ Activity One

Direction: In this section, you will hear a long passage. After listening, you should choose the best answer to each question. Now listen to the passage.

1. What does Nick Bostrom point out in his book *Superintelligence*?

    A. AI has a positive influence on the future development of humankind.

B. AI has a creative effect on the high-tech science.

C. AI will pose a threat to mankind.

D. AI will produce a potential risk to commercial development.

2. According to Nick Bostrom, what will AI show if it chooses actions based on achieving some goal?

   A. It will exhibit positive behavior.   **B.** It will show convergent behavior.

   C. It will protect itself from being opened up.   **D.** It will protect itself from being start-up.

3. If the existential danger was realized, what would the hypothetical AI do?

   A. It would have to overpower or out-think all of humanity.

   B. It would be an unworthy research.

   C. It would be developed within the power of humanity.

   D. It would not go far from the current level.

4. Which company is **NOT** mentioned funded by Musk to develop AI?

   A. Google.   **B.** DeepMind.

   C. Baidu.   **D.** Vicarious.

5. What is the related concern about AI?

   A. Developing militarized artificial intelligence.

   B. The development of battlefield robots.

   C. The development of super intelligent AI.

   D. Developing artificial soldiers.

② Activity Two

Direction: Listen again and decide whether the following statements are true (T) or false (F).

6. A universal concern about the development of artificial intelligence is the existential threat that could pose to mankind. (   )

7. A group of prominent tech titans have donated $1 billion to OpenAI. (   )

8. Concern over risk from military artificial intelligence has led to some high-profile donations and investments. (   )

9. In January 2015, Elon Musk donated 1,000,000 dollars to the Future of Life Institute to fund research on understanding AI decision making. (   )

10. Currently, more than 50 countries are researching battlefield robots, including China, the United States, the United Kingdom, and Russia. (   )

Text B The Development of Approaches to AI Research

⚙ Vocabulary

unify	['junɪfaɪ]	*vt.*	form (something) into a single unit or make uniform 使统一；使一致；使成为一体
optimization	[ˌɑptəmɪ'zeʃən]	*n.*	the act of making something as good as possible 最佳化；最优化
coin	[kɔɪn]	*vt.*	invent a new word or expression 创造（新词语）
synthetic	[sɪn'θetɪk]	*adj.*	Synthetic products are made from artificial substances, often copying a natural product. 合成的；人造的
computational	[ˌkɑmpjʊ'teʃəl]	*n.*	using or connected with computers 使用计算机的；与计算机有关的
mimic	['mɪmɪk]	*vt.*	copy the way in which a particular person usually speaks and moves, usually in order to make people laugh 模仿
essence	['ɛsns]	*n.*	the basic or most important idea or quality of something 本质；精华
previous	['privɪəs]	*adj.*	happening or existing before something or someone else 以前的；早先的
cybernetics	[ˌsaɪbɚ'nɛtɪks]	*n.*	the scientific study of how information is communicated in machines and electronic devices 控制学；人机关系学
symbolic	[sɪm'bɑlɪk]	*adj.*	(of something) containing symbols, or being used as a symbol 象征的；符号的
simulation	[ˌsɪmjə'leʃən]	*n.*	a situation in which a particular set of conditions is created artificially in order to study or experience something that could exist in reality 仿真；模拟

| formalize | ['fɔrməlaɪz] | vt. | give something a fixed structure or form by introducing rules 使形式化 |
| programming | ['progræmɪŋ] | n. | the activity or job of writing computer programs 编制程序 |

❶ Activity One

*Direction: In this section, you will hear a passage **ONLY ONCE**. While listening, you may write **NO MORE THAN THREE WORDS** for each gap. Make sure the word(s) you fill in is (are) both grammatically and semantically acceptable. Now listen to the passage.*

The Development of Approaches to AI Research

Should artificial intelligence **1.** _____ natural intelligence by studying psychology or **2.** _____? John Haugeland proposed that AI should more properly be referred to as **3.** _____. According to Stuart Shapiro, there are three approaches of AI research: **4.** _____, computational philosophy and computer science. Computational philosophy is used to develop an **5.** _____, free-flowing computer mind.

In the 1940s and 1950s, some researchers built machines that used **6.** _____ to exhibit rudimentary intelligence. By 1960, this approach was largely discarded, although elements of it would be **7.** _____ in the 1980s.

In the middle 1950s, AI research began to explore the possibility that human intelligence could be reduced to symbol **8.** _____. Approaches based on cybernetics or neural networks were **9.** _____ or pushed into the background. Researchers in the 1960s and the 1970s were convinced that **10.** _____ would eventually be a success.

❷ Activity Two

Direction: Listen again and decide whether the following statements are true (T) or false (F).

11. Practicing computer science goes for the goal of creating computers that can perform tasks that other species could previously accomplish. (   )

12. In the 1940s and 1950s, many researchers explored the relation between neurology and information theory. (   )

13. In 1970s, economist Herbert Simon and Allen Newell laid the foundations of the field of artificial intelligence, as well as cognitive science, operations research and management science. (   )

14. John McCarthy felt that it was unnecessary for machines to simulate human thought, but they should try to find the essence of abstract reasoning and problem solving. (　　)

15. Logic was also the minor point of the work at the University of Edinburgh and elsewhere in Europe which contributed to the development of the programming language Prolog and the science of logic programming. (　　)

Post-Listening

Direction: Work in pairs and discuss the following questions.

1. What do you think of applying AI to develop man-like machine?

2. Is it threatening to further develop AI? Why or why not?

Section B Speaking

Expressing Thanks in a Thank-you Speech

When you receive an award or an honor, you might be called upon the stage to give a thank-you speech. A thank-you speech is a short public speech, which serves to express gratitude for something that was presented or offered to a person as a spiritual gift (love, support, help, personal time, caring attitude) or material one (a tangible article).

A thank-you speech is a chance to express how sincerely grateful you are to the people who helped you along the way, and perhaps share a funny story or two to make your audience smile.

A thank-you speech usually follows the structure as follows:

Start with an expression of gratitude for the award. You can start by saying thank you for the award or honor you're receiving by saying something like "I'm so honored to be here tonight, and grateful to be the recipient of this award."

Express thanks and respect for the people honoring you. You need to express your sincere regard and gratefulness for the people who are giving you the award. For example, if you're being honored by your company, talk about the great work the company does, and what a pleasure it is to work there.

Mention the names of the people who have helped you. You also need to give credit to the people whose support has helped you accomplish something worth honoring. Make a short list of the names of your colleagues, friends and family members without whose help you wouldn't be receiving this honor. Try not to leave anyone important off your list, but you don't need to list everyone you know, either. Keep it limited to people who actually helped you.

Highlight the personal significance of the award. Before you end your thank-you speech, you can say a few words about how this award has made your efforts worthwhile, or how it will encourage you to continue working hard, etc. so that the speech can end on an inspiring note.

Moreover, every part of a thank-you speech may be vividly illustrated by real life stories. It's both charming and entertaining to tell an anecdote or two about something that happened leading up to the honor you're receiving. Since thank-you speeches are often given at dinners and festive events, saying something to keep the mood light and bring smiles to people's faces will be appreciated.

A thank-you speech should be distinctly articulated, brief and focused. Proper articulation and audibility are especially important for a thank-you speech because faltering and muttering may seem close to hesitation and lack of sincerity. Brevity is also required since lengthy speeches are often tiresome and the message may lose its focus.

Questions to Think About

1. Has there ever been any occasion in your life where you need to publicly thank someone? What was the occasion like?

2. Many celebrities, such as movie stars and famous business people, have made thank-you speeches for awards they receive. Find some thank-you speeches given by celebrities and decide which one you like best. In what way do you think it is impressive or memorable?

3. Are there any differences between a thank-you speech in English and one in Chinese? If yes, what are the differences?

4. In mentioning all the names of the people who have helped you, whose name should come first? Or, how would you order and organize people's names?

Communication Tasks

1. On March 15, 2016, Google's artificial intelligence program AlphaGo was awarded the highest Go grandmaster rank, before AlphaGo won the final game of the five-match series with South Korean grandmaster Lee SeDol. The highest Go grandmaster rank is reserved for those whose

ability at the ancient board game borders on "divinity". This award represents the greatest recognition of the development of artificial intelligence. If you were AlphaGo, whom would you thank and what would you say in a thank-you speech after winning this award?

2. On June 21, 2016, the Invention and Entrepreneurship Award in Robotics and Automation was presented to Phil Crowther, for the collaborative dual-arm robot YuMi. The name stands for "you and me—we work together". Find out more information about YuMi and the story behind its invention. Then compose a thank-you speech for YuMi as the recipient of the 2016 Invention and Entrepreneurship Award.

3. Suppose you are at your 20th birthday party. You want to express your thanks to all the people who have made your life possible and meaningful—your parents, friends, teachers, classmates, etc. Compose a thank-you speech and deliver it to your classmates.

Section  Exam Spotlight

① Activity One

*Direction: In this section, you will hear a conversation. For questions 1–2, you should choose the best answer to each question. For questions 3–10, you should complete the notes below with **NO MORE THAN THREE WORDS** for each answer.*

1. **A.** Violence on television.

   B. Transportation in the city.

   C. The history of transportation.

2. **A.** Everyone thinks there is too much violence on TV.

   B. There is no real agreement on the amount of violence.

   C. Most people think there is too much violence on TV.

   Most people think that violent programs should only be shown **3.** _____.

   Most people felt that violence on **4.** _____ is more acceptable for it is important to keep in touch with **5.** _____.

Frank gave out 120 copies and got **6.** _____ back, but Theresa says his survey **7.** _____ public opinion.

Theresa plans to go to interview her respondents in the **8.** _____ by asking **9.** _____ so that she can select people of all **10.** _____
_____ .

② Activity Two

Direction: In this section, you will hear a passage. For questions 11–16, you should match the columns below. For questions 17–20, you should decide whether the statements are true (T) or false (F).

11. The Arctic Region _____   **A.** The climate is continental, with clear seasonal change.

12. The Northern Region _____   **B.** Yellowknife is in this region.

13. The Prairie Region _____   **C.** It has short summer and severe winter.

14. The Cordillera Region _____   **D.** The weather is always pleasant.

15. The Pacific Region _____   **E.** The weather is often snowy and windy.

16. The Southeastern Region _____   **F.** It has adequate rainfall.

17. The climate can be very different in different regions. (   )

18. The winter in the Arctic Region may last for six months. (   )

19. The driest region is the Prairie Region. (   )

20. The warmest city of Canada is in the Pacific Region. (   )

③ Activity Three

*Direction: In this section, you will hear a passage **THREE TIMES**. When the passage is read for the first time, you should listen carefully for its general idea. When the passage is read for the second time, you are required to fill in the blanks with the exact words you have just heard. Finally, when the passage is read for the third time, you should check what you have written.*

A nuclear family is **21.** _____ in highly-industrialized societies. Beginning in the early 20th century, the two-parent family **22.** _____ as the nuclear family was the predominant American family type. **23.** _____, children live with their parents until they go away to a college or university, or until they **24.** _____ jobs and acquire an **25.** _____ or home of their own.

In the early mid-20th century, the father was typically the **26.** _____ wage-earner, and the mother was the children's **27.** _____ caregiver. Today, often both parents **28.** _____ jobs. **29.** _____. Increasingly, one of the parents has a non-standard shift, that is, a shift that does not start in the morning and end in the late afternoon. In these families, one of the parents manages the children while the other works. Prior to school, **30.** _____

_____.

In recent years, many private companies and home-based day care centers have sprung up to fulfill this need. Increasingly, **31.** _____

_____. Governments are providing assistance to parents that require day care as well.

---

④ Activity Four

*Direction: In this section, you will hear a conversation **ONLY ONCE**. After listening, you should answer the following questions. Now listen to the conversation.*

32. What's the main point of this conversation?

33. According to the man, when will the River Valley tour take place?

34. Will Miss Schmidt rent a bicycle from the tour center?

35. Does Miss Schmidt have some diet restrictions? Why or why not?

Unit 15
Virtual Reality

Learning Objectives

- To get to know general information of virtual reality
- To learn technical words concerning virtual reality
- To learn to listen for stress in listening materials
- To learn to tell stories and experiences

Section **A** Listening

Pre-Listening

Direction: Work in pairs and discuss the following questions.

1. What is VR? What do you know about VR?

2. Have you ever had VR experiences? What do you think of it?

Warm-up Activities

⚙ Vocabulary

sue	[su]	*vt.*	institute legal proceedings against; file a suit against 起诉；控告
automotive	[ˌɔtə'motɪv]	*adj.*	of or relating to motor vehicles 汽车的
marine	[mə'rin]	*adj.*	of or relating to the sea 海洋的
interdisciplinary	[ˌɪntə'dɪsəplɪnɛrɪ]	*adj.*	drawing from or characterized by participation of two or more fields of study 跨学科的

① Activity One

Direction: In this section, you will hear a passage. After listening, you should decide whether the following statements are true (T) or false (F). Now listen to the passage.

1. Game rules are the same with those of the real world. (   )

2. When you're cheated or hurt, or mistreated by someone, you can go to the city affairs office to sue him or her. (   )

3. Gambling is no longer a sin since it is virtual money you win or lose. (   )

② Activity Two

Direction: Listen to another passage and choose the best answer to each question.

4. When was the Virtual Reality Laboratory (VRL) at the College of Engineering founded in the University of Michigan?

   A. In 1991.   **B.** In 1992.

   C. In 1993.   **D.** In 1994.

5. Initially, what does the research at the VRL focus on?

   A. Agricultural applications.   **B.** Industrial applications.

   C. IT applications.   **D.** Business applications.

6. Virtual reality has been used in many areas, except in _____.

   A. Accident simulations.   **B.** Medicine.

   C. Architecture.   **D.** Marine industry.

While-Listening

Text A Cutting a Frog Through "Virtual Dissection"

⚙ Vocabulary

dissection	[dɪˈsɛkʃən]	*n.*	cutting so as to separate into pieces 切割；解剖
formaldehyde	[fɔrˈmældɪhaɪd]	*n.*	strong-smelling colorless gas used as a preservative and disinfectant when dissolved in water 甲醛
demonstration	[ˌdɛmənˈstreʃən]	*n.*	(instance of) showing and explaining how something works 示范；证明
wireless	[ˈwaɪɚləs]	*adj.*	having no wires 不用电线的

① Activity One

Direction: In this section, you will hear a long passage. After listening, you should choose the best answer to each question. Now listen to the passage.

1. What does the company called Froguts sell to schools?

   A. Frogs.   **B.** Educational services.

   C. Computers.   **D.** Cutting tools.

2. Which is **NOT** mentioned as the place children can still "visit" by computer?

   A. Zoos.   **B.** Museums.

   C. Movie theaters.   **D.** Historic places.

3. In Maine, how many schools have wireless computers now?

   A. More than 240.   **B.** More than 270.

   C. Less than 270.   **D.** More than 280.

4. In Michigan, how much should schools pay for each student to get the computers?

   A. 23 dollars.   **B.** 24 dollars.

   C. 25 dollars.   **D.** 26 dollars.

5. Other teachers say the computer is simply another tool. What does the tool depend on?

   A. Who uses it.   **B.** How much it is.

   C. What it is used for.   **D.** How it is used.

② Activity Two

Direction: Listen again and decide whether the following statements are true (T) or false (F).

6. Some schools no longer require students to cut apart frogs just because of the cost. (   )

7. A company called Froguts sells demonstrations to schools. (   )

8. All educators say nothing can replace the real thing. (   )

9. Distance and money may prevent some students from going to places like museums and zoos. (   )

10. Michigan has started to spend $22,000,000 for laptop or hand-held computers for seventh graders. (   )

Text B Are You Ready for Virtual Reality?

⚙ Vocabulary

zany	['zenɪ]	*adj.*	ludicrous, foolish 滑稽的，可笑的
snapshot	['snæpʃɑt]	*n.*	a short description or a small amount of information that gives you an idea of what something is like 简介
acquisition	[ˌækwɪ'zɪʃən]	*n.*	the act of contracting or assuming or acquiring possession of something 收购
dazed	[dezd]	*adj.*	in a state of mental numbness 眩晕的
fidelity	[fɪ'dɛlətɪ]	*n.*	accuracy with which an electronic system reproduces the sound or image of its input signal 逼真度；保真
discrepancy	[dɪs'krɛpənsɪ]	*n.*	difference 差别
panoramic	[ˌpænə'ræmɪk]	*adj.*	an impressive view of a wide are a of land 全景的，全貌的
escapism	[ɪ'skepɪzəm]	*n.*	an inclination to retreat from unpleasant realities through diversion or fantasy 逃避现实

① Activity One

Direction: In this section, you will hear a long passage. After listening, you should decide whether the following statements are true (T) or false (F). Now listen to the passage.

1. Jeremy Bailenson worries about whether VR will be accepted by the mainstream. (   )

2. Tadhg Kelly has been skeptical of VR's ability to go mainstream. (   )

3. Chris Dixon said it was not at the right time for all the stuff to work. (   )

4. The author found it incredibly difficult to bend his head down and touch one of the people nose to nose. (   )

5. According to Mr. Dixon, people wouldn't want to use Oculus to look at a panoramic photo after a long day of work — to change their mental state by escaping into a photo. (   )

② Activity Two

Direction: Listen again and choose the best answer to each question.

6. Which of the following statements is **NOT** the reason for "Virtual reality is coming, and you're going to jump into it"?

    A. Virtual reality is the natural extension of every major technology we use today—of movies, TV, video-conferencing, the smart phone and the web.

    B. Virtual reality is the ultra-immersive version of the major technologies we use today.

    C. Virtual reality will even alter how society deals with such weighty issues as gender parity and environmental destruction.

    D. We'll use virtual reality exactly the same ways—to communicate, to learn, and to entertain ourselves and escape.

7. For years, what was the most convincing criticism of virtual reality?

    A. It can make people dazed.

    B. It can play strange tricks on one's body, mind and mood.

    C. It can make people be hooked on it.

    D. It just wouldn't be good enough.

8. How do virtual reality devices work?

    A. By offering a far more realistic simulation.

    B. By running test subjects through the lab's technology.

    C. By sending a computer-generated image to each of your eyes in response to your movements.

    D. By seeing how people respond to virtual environments.

9. What does the simulator's fidelity depend on?

    A. How clearly it can track your image.

    B. How quickly it can track your image.

    C. How accurately it can track your movements and how quickly it can adjust the image to match the motion.

    D. How clearly it can track your movements.

10. According to the researchers, why can virtual meetings be even better than real-life encounters?

    A. Because it lets us feel a sense of human connection.

    B. Because our avatars can be programmed to act perfectly manipulatively, in ways that we can't.

C. Because face-to-face meetings are powerful.

D. Because virtual reality is a powerful communications platform.

Post-Listening

Direction: Work in pairs and discuss the following questions.

1. Do you have any dreams that you think VR might help you realize? Why do you have that dream?

2. What's your opinion about virtual dissection?

Section B Speaking

Telling Your Own Story or Experiences

When a speaker uses stories the audience has heard before, her or his credibility is needlessly affected in a negative way. Old stories can also take away the impact the speech would otherwise have. An effective way of avoiding telling stale trash stories is that you can use your own story or personal experiences rather than fishing a story out of an anthology or a magazine, or, even worse, repeating one you heard another speaker use. When you relate to your own professional or personal experience as examples, the material is personal and uniquely yours, and it may add to the interest and impact of your speech. This is why professional presenters regularly use stories, especially personal ones, in their presentations and publications.

When you turn personal experiences into stories to tell, it's important that you remember that sharing such experiences requires you to be willing to talk publicly about what are essentially private events. You need to make sure that you feel comfortable doing so. This may take some practice. But once you become comfortable sharing personal stories, you can move on and adapt experiences of a wide range and create various stories for your presentations and speeches.

From now on, you can get into the habit of writing down your experiences that can be applied to the principles you believe in or talk about to others. As the old saying goes, "Don't think it, ink it." In a few years you will have a wealth of illustrative material drawn from your own personal experiences.

If you don't have years of experience to draw from, you can collect stories from a variety of sources, or "borrow" the experience from someone else in your area who does have experiences to share. For example, if you need a case study to illustrate customer satisfaction, ask an experienced colleague to tell you his or her best example to satisfy a customer. Then tell the story in your speech and give credit to the source. Such stories have a strong sense of reality and can create direct impact.

When you tell a story, choose only the best detail, that is, details that are most directly relevant to your point and at the same time interesting to most audience. In other words, there is no need to include everything that happened in the experience. You may also use description and dialogue to add spice to your story.

Story-telling, as a part of your speech or presentation, can immensely help to illustrate reality and clarify a point. It can also provide humor, make points memorable, build a shared vision, encourage thinking and inspire people to act. It is worth all your efforts to practice and to become a better story-teller.

Questions to Think About

1. What are the advantages of using your own story or experience in your speech?

2. How can you decide whether a personal experience will be suitable for a certain occasion?

3. Would there be any differences between using your own experiences and using someone else's experiences?

4. How can you decide what details to include in your story, and what details to omit?

Communication Tasks

1. Do you have any novel experiences, such as trying new food, or travelling in a foreign country, that you can share with your classmates? Tell about such an experience to your classmates.

2. Have you ever learned an important life lesson from a personal experience? What was that experience? And what was the lesson that you learned from it? Tell this to your classmates.

3. Have you played interactive games on a computer? What was the experience like? Tell about this experience to one of your classmates who has not played this kind of game. Try to let him/ her experience the game through your experience.

Section  Exam Spotlight

① Activity One

*Direction: In this section, you will hear a telephone conversation in which Frances Drew asks Mr. Harding about Arts Club. After listening, you should fill in the blanks. Write **NO MORE THAN THREE WORDS** for each answer.*

Arts Club Secretary—Tel.363

Example:

Calendar—collect from library on <u>Thursday</u>

Membership fee **1.** _____ per adult

Social events:

Club evenings take place **2.** _____

at the Beach Pavilion, **3.** _____

Choir practices held on **4.** _____

To join the choir, apply through **5.** _____

Name of the treasurer who deals with the fee **6.** _____

Cheque payable to **7.** _____

Members receive **8.** _____ three times a year

Activities sections:

Acting group—The Players

Musical activities: Choir and **9.** _____

Literary and discussion groups

Studio Workshop, Arts Talk and **10.** _____

➁ Activity Two

Direction: In this section, you will hear an interview about the International Space Station. After listening, you should choose the best answer(s) to each question.

11. A. 20.   **B.** 15.   **C.** 5.

12. A. $128 billion.   **B.** $120 billion.   **C.** $8 billion.

13. A. By using very little.

     B. By recycling all the water.

     C. By transporting plenty from Earth.

14. (Choose Three Answers)

     A. Plant cultivation.   **B.** Mapping.

     C. Solar energy.   **D.** Weather patterns.

     E. Studies in low gravity.   **F.** Psychology.

     G. Nutrition.

15. (Choose Two Answers)

     A. Turning on the computers.   **B.** Attending meetings.

     C. Cooking breakfast.   **D.** Physical exercise.

     E. Listening to CDs.   **F.** Communicating with family.

➂ Activity Three

*Direction: In this section, you will hear a passage. After listening, you should complete the notes below. Write **NO MORE THAN THREE WORDS** for each answer.*

General History

- The Aztec empire existed between the **16.** _____ century.

- The **17.** _____ of Aztec was in the center of the modern Mexico City.

Food

- The staple food of the Aztec empire was **18.** _____ which has been domesticated for thousands of years, and spread to the rest of the world from Mexico.

- **19.** _____ are also part of the Aztec diet.

Clothing

- The clothing of the Aztec was diverse based on different **20.** _____.

- Aztec clothes were generally made of imported cotton or ayate fiber.

- The Aztecs were able to create beautiful colors using a lot of **21.** _____.

Education

- Girls were instructed about cooking, caring for a family, **22.** _____ and ways to economically run the home.

- Boys, however, learned trades, fighting skills and **23.** _____ skills.

Religion

- The Aztecs went to temples to **24.** _____ and send their tribute.

- The tribute included not only agricultural produce but also **25.** _____ goods.

④ Activity Four

*Direction: In this section, you will hear a passage **ONLY ONCE**. After listening, you should fill in the blanks. Now listen to the passage.*

Natural Resources

Through the changes in the ways of making a living in a family over several **26.** _____, the cartoon aims at sounding a warning against man's wasteful use of natural resources and emphasizing the **27.** _____ need to **28.** _____ these resources.

Ever since man appeared on the Earth, man's **29.** _____ has been heavily dependent on nature. Almost everything we use in our everyday life comes from nature, ranging from the food we eat, the water we drink, to the wood which is turned into **30.** _____. With the development of technology and population growth, the amount and range of materials used has increased at an **31.** _____ rate.

However, natural resources are not inexhaustible. Some **32.** _____ are already on the brink of **33.** _____ and there is no hope of replacing them. The widespread water shortage is an example in point. If man continued to **34.** _____ natural resources with no thought for the future, the whole world would be in a **35.** _____.

Unit 16
Digital Darwinism

Learning Objectives

- To learn basic knowledge of digital Darwinism
- To learn to introduce the digital development
- To learn skills of summarizing and retelling

Section **A** Listening

Pre-Listening

Direction: Work in pairs and discuss the following questions.

1. What do you think of digital Darwinism?

2. How does the digital Darwinism impact the business circle?

Warm-up Activities

⚙ Vocabulary

Interactive Advertising Bureau (IAB)			美国互动广告局
American Association of Advertising Agencies (AAAA)			美国广告代理商协会
HP			惠普公司
morph	[mɔrf]	*vt.*	develop a new appearance or change into something else, or make something do this 转化为，变成
on (a) par with			equal in importance, quality, etc. 与……同等重要、同等水平
purview	['pɜˑvju]	*n.*	range of operation or activity（工作或活动的）范围
distinguished	[dɪ'stɪŋgwɪʃt]	*adj.*	successful, respected, and admired 卓越的；受人尊敬的
landmark	['lændmɑrk]	*n.*	one of the most important events, changes, or discoveries that influences someone or something 里程碑
arena	[ə'rinə]	*n.*	place or scene of activity or conflict 活动或斗争的场所或场面
comprehensive	[ˌkɑmprɪ'hɛnsɪv]	*adj.*	complete and including everything that is necessary 综合的；全面的

① Activity One

Direction: In this section, you will hear a passage. After listening, you should choose the best answer to each question. Now listen to the passage.

1. Which part is **NOT** mentioned in the reshaped relationships?

   A. Marketers.   **B.** Media companies.

   C. Advertising agencies.   **D.** Businessmen.

2. What's the key point of digital Darwinism?

   A. Survival of losers.

   B. Survival of winners distinguished from losers.

   C. Distinguishing losers from winners.

   D. Distinguishing losers from the fittest.

3. What has upended the traditional relationship between companies and consumers?

   A. Multiparty.   **B.** Multimedia.

   C. Web 2.0.   **D.** Digital conversations.

② Activity Two

Direction: Listen again and decide whether the following statements are true (T) or false (F).

4. Mendenhall knows that digital platforms and capabilities are now transforming ways that will give consumers a real experience in advertising. (   )

5. The ecosystem, a complex and interconnected community, is a proper simile for nowadays business environment. (   )

6. When companies have special characteristics in their whole organizational structure or excellent skills of self-adaptation, they are bound to success in a marketing environment of "digital Darwinism". (   )

While-Listening

Text A The Impact of Digital Platform

⚙ Vocabulary

nurture	['nɜːtʃə]	*vt.*	take care of, feed, and protect someone or something, especially young children or plants, and help him, her, or it to develop 养育
aggregator	['ægrɪgetə]	*n.*	a website or computer software that aggregates a specific type of information from multiple online sources 集合器
glean	[glin]	*vt.*	collect information in small amounts and often with difficulty 收集；搜集
ingredient	[ɪn'gridɪənt]	*n.*	any of the qualities of which something is made 因素；要素；成分

❶ Activity One

Direction: In this section, you will hear a long passage. After listening, you should choose the best answer to each question. Now listen to the passage.

1. According to Mendenhall, what is **NOT** mentioned about digital formats and platforms in its redefinition?

    A. HP's relationships with external marketing partners.

    B. External opportunities.

    C. Internal organization.

    D. Internal capabilities.

2. Why are marketers responsible to boost change within their companies?

    A. Because most digitalized touch points exert impact on them.

    B. Because all public touch points follow the traditional way.

    C. Because it is the request from the brand campaigns.

    D. Because new opportunities are fewer than before.

3. What's the result of the "Marketing & Media Ecosystem 2010" study?

    A. Nearly 450 professionals are ignorant of the survey's questions.

    B. More than 75 senior executives disagree to receive further interviews.

    C. It has yielded valuable insights on the gaps and gold mines in today's landscape.

    D. It makes more people focus on the priorities, capabilities and partnerships.

4. How many touch point do the Yahoo, Walt Disney, and *New York Times* have accordingly?

    A. 60, 811, 45.   **B.** 118, 16, 45.

    C. 811, 16, 45.   **D.** 811, 60, 45.

5. What has the marketing function changed into?

    A. Broadcasting brand messages to consumers.

    B. A center for dialogue.

    C. Making more advertisements to attract customers.

    D. A closely connected digital ecosystem.

❷ Activity Two

Direction: Listen again and decide whether the following statements are true (T) or false (F).

6. According to Mendenhall, it is campaign that determines brands, not the consumer ecosystems. (   )

7. Those platforms and capabilities have a visible impact on every aspect of the marketing process and brand experience. (   )

8. Over 415 professionals in the related areas responded to the questions about the trends that would remold the industry by 2010. (   )

9. As knowing more consumer preferences, Google, Microsoft, AOL, MySpace and Facebook can get a good control of their audiences, better matching ads to consumer segments. (   )

10. In the marketing model which "listens and learns", relevance, interactivity and accountability have weighed so much. (   )

Text B What Is Tendency Under the Digital Darwinism?

⚙ Vocabulary

enthusiast	[ɪnˈθuːziæst]	*n.*	a person who is very interested in and involved with a particular subject or activity 狂热者，爱好者
continuous	[kənˈtɪnjʊəs]	*adj.*	without a pause or interruption 连续的；继续的
Bogota		*n.*	波哥大（哥伦比亚首都）
Sao Paulo		*n.*	圣保罗（巴西城市）
Munich		*n.*	慕尼黑（德国城市）
Seoul		*n.*	首尔（韩国首都）

① Activity One

*Direction: In this section, you will hear the first part of a passage **ONLY ONCE**. While listening, you may write **NO MORE THAN THREE WORDS** for each gap. Make sure the word(s) you fill in is (are) both grammatically and semantically acceptable. Now listen to the passage.*

What Is Tendency Under the Digital Darwinism?

As the physical event literally moved across the globe, digital media enthusiasts **1.** _____ its progress live online. As Hidalgo noted that our revenue went up and it presented how we could combine consumers' **2.** _____ experiences to make a more powerful linkage.

Place context **3.** _____ content. The distribution of their timing, context and **4.** _____ is very important. **5.** _____, marketers tend to raise the profile of media strategy and plan within their organizations. Marketers begin to shift their **6.** _____ strategies so as to build capabilities in communication planning.

7. _____ one-fifth of the marketers in our study have invested in internal communication planning functions. Those that plan, **8.** _____ their media buys are becoming important partners with marketers.

Associated with this major point on the media mix is the demand for greater **9.** _____ and speed. In fact, most marketers said that media will be bought and sold on a real-time, **10.** _____ and continuous basis.

② Activity Two

Direction: Listen to the rest of the passage and answer the following questions in your own words.

11. What is the major obstacle to the whole ecosystem's transition to a new marketing and media model?

12. Why do leading marketers build relationships with digital agencies and other media companies?

13. What helps marketers assess the total return on their expenditure in MTV's media properties?

14. What has the linear value chain been replaced with?

Post-Listening

Direction: Work in pairs and discuss the following questions.

1. Does it make any sense for companies to struggle to transform their business models? Why or why not?

2. Is it useful for companies to cooperate with other media companies? Why or why not?

Section B Speaking

Summarizing and Retelling

The ability to summarize is essential in an age of information explosion where various data is overflowing and overwhelming. You may need to summarize business reports, sales results, market conditions, industry news, events and procedures, etc. for the purpose of reporting them briefly to directors or colleagues, or you may keep a short note of such information for you own reference.

Usually a summary should be approximately 1/4 the length of the original material, or even less, without sacrificing the key information. A summary usually includes the following three parts: 1) information about the source or the author; 2) a gist of the content of the original material (book, news, report, procedure, etc.); 3) your own interpretation or comments (optional). Giving a summary means reprocessing the information, which includes comprehension, capturing, reorganizing, and representing.

Comprehension: In order to write an accurate summary, you must read the original material to be summarized thoroughly and make sure you completely understand it. You need to look for the thesis given by the author and highlight it, and you can also highlight the key points, such as subheadings and topic sentences, while you are reading.

Capturing: This means that you should be able to identify all the major points and recognize the relationships between and among them. Particular attention needs to be paid to the information concerning the wh-questions: when, where, who, what, how, why, etc. Examples or detailed descriptions should not mislead you or confuse you. If there is comparison and contrast between the points, or a cause-effect relationship, or a complementary relationship, etc., you should be able to recognize it. Capturing the key points and sorting out the relationships between them will enable you to outline all the information presented in the original piece, and this lead you to a clear and effective skeleton of your summary.

Reorganizing: Although you need to summarize the original piece as a whole, you may or may not follow the structure of the original piece. Your principle should be retelling all major points in a straightforward, easy-to-follow order. You should omit nothing important and clearly indicate the relationships between each point. If you reorganize the information, you should strive for overall coherence through using appropriate transitions. At the end, conclude with a statement reflecting the author's standpoint and the significance of the original piece.

Representing: Start by telling your audience you are summarizing and remember to identify the source material — author, title, etc. Use summarizing language like "The figures show that" or "This analysis claims that", and present the main points neutrally. If you believe there are points that are extremely important and cannot be reworded, you can quote and repeat the statement from the original. You may paraphrase and use your own language, but you need to be faithful to the original message. So you should be accurate and concise at the same time.

Questions to Think About

1. When it comes to summarizing and retelling, how "brief" do you believe is really brief? Why?

2. Where can you usually find the thesis of an article?

3. Why is it important to recognize the relationships between the major points in the original material?

4. In doing summary, should you always try to paraphrase and use your own word, or stick to the original wording?

5. What do you think is the most difficult part of summarizing?

Communication Tasks

1. Find an article titled "Digital Darwinism: How Disruptive Technology Is Changing Business for Good" on the Internet, and give a summary of this article to your classmates.

2. What movie have you seen recently? Retell the plot of the movie to one of your classmates who has not seen it. Make sure that your summary and retelling will make sense to your classmates.

3. What book have you read recently? Tell your classmates about it and present a book summary to your class in 2 minutes.

Section C Exam Spotlight

Activity One

Direction: In this section, you will hear a conversation. For questions 1–5, you should decide whether the statements are true (T) or false (F). For questions 6–10, you should fill in the blanks with proper words or phrases.

1. The two speakers want to rent a house close to the university. (   )

2. The man cannot bear small flat. (   )

3. The man doesn't mind living in a noisy area. But he thinks a quieter place is better. (   )

4. They are not students and they don't care about the rent. (   )

5. They surf on the Internet to find the house they need. (   )

6. Absolutely! That's the most important thing to _____.

7. I am not too worried about _____.

8. I'm not _____ . But quieter is better for _____ .

9. Let's go to _____ and see what they can offer us.

10. I think you had a good idea to start _____ early.

② Activity Two

Direction: In this section, you will hear five short recordings. For each recording, you should decide the speaker's attitude toward meeting. Choose one letter (A–H) from the box next to each blank. Do not use any letter more than once.

A. Everyone should play an active role in the meeting.

B. He shows negative attitude toward meetings.

C. We should arrange different types of meetings.

D. Meeting can be very fruitful.

E. Meeting helps us interact with others.

F. Meeting helps to improve market share.

G. We should arrange meeting agendas.

H. It is advised to increase the frequency of meetings.

11. _____

12. _____

13. _____

14. _____

15. _____

③ Activity Three

*Direction: In this section, you will hear a passage **THREE TIMES**. When the passage is read for the first time, you should listen carefully for its general idea. When the passage is read for the second time, you are required to fill in the blanks with the exact words you have just heard. Finally, when the passage is read for the third time, you should check what you have written.*

Putting feelings into words makes sadness and anger less intense, U.S. brain researchers said on Wednesday, in a finding that explains why talking to a therapist often makes people feel better.

They said talking about negative feelings **16.** _____ a part of the brain responsible for impulse control. "This region of the brain seems to **17.** _____ putting on the brakes," said researcher Matthew Lieberman. He and his colleagues **18.** _____ the brains of 30 people—18 women and 12 men between 18 and 36—who were shown pictures of faces **19.** _____ strong emotions. They were asked to **20.** _____ the feelings in words like "sad" or "angry", or to choose between two gender-specific names like "Sally" or "Harry" that matched the face.

What they found is that when people **21.** _____ a word like "angry" to an angry-looking face, the **22.** _____ in the portion of the brain that handles fear, panic and other strong emotions decreased. "This seems to dampen down the response in this basic emotional circuit in the brain," Lieberman said in a telephone interview.

The researchers did not find **23.** _____ differences along gender lines, but Lieberman said prior studies had hinted at some differences in the benefits men and women **24.** _____ talking about their feelings. "Women may do more of this **25.** _____ , but when men are instructed to do it, they may get more benefit from it," he said.

❹ Activity Four

*Direction: In this section, you will hear a conversation **ONLY ONCE**. While listening, you may write **NO MORE THAN THREE WORDS** for each gap. Make sure the word(s) you fill in is (are) both grammatically and semantically acceptable. Now listen to the conversation.*

Job Enquiry
• Type of work: **26.** _____
• Number of hours per week: **27.** _____
• Work in the **28.** _____ branch
• Nearest bus stop: Next to **29.** _____
• Pay: **30.** _____ an hour
• Extra benefits:
a) a free dinner
b) extra pay when you work on **31.** _____
c) transport home when you work **32.** _____

- Qualities required:
  a) **33.** _____

  b) ability to **34.** _____
- Interview arranged for: Thursday **35.** _____ at 6 p.m.

Glossary

(Text A=A; Text B=B; Warm-up=W)

A

B

C

resistor	Unit 13B
reveal	Unit 1W
rigorous	Unit 2W
roam	Unit 7A
robe	Unit 13W
ROM (Read Only Memory)	Unit 3A
roughly	Unit 9A
router	Unit 5B

S

sample	Unit 8A
Sao Paulo	Unit 16B
SAT (Scholastic Aptitude Test)	Unit 4A
sedentary	Unit 7W
sensitive	Unit 7W
Seoul	Unit 16B
sensor	Unit 9B
server	Unit 5B
simulation	Unit 14B
slide	Unit 8B
snapshot	Unit 15B
Snow Leopard	Unit 3A
societal	Unit 3W
soothe	Unit 7B
spotty	Unit 6A
spurt	Unit 9W
spreadsheet	Unit 4A
SSL (Security Socket Layer)	Unit 6B
statistically	Unit 6W
staggering	Unit 6A
stakeholder	Unit 10A

T